The whole world was under bondage under the 'Transatlantic slave t
Arab state zenith tribe faced disintegration and cope thru time Darwin's survival of the
fittest was a pilgrim Joseph Smith Family of wealth and power, my grandmother
strived corn beef, poor blacks married west indies lateral Indian caste system, the
poorer the blacker vegetable growers.

- Tithe , offering is to GROW CHURCH is God well pleased investing in things of God is creating heirs , will surely be blessed MALACHI 3:10.

- Song of Pharaoh Africa – Praise and Worship Song,

- Dedication to Dr Pastor Ian Thurlby Campbell and our multiple children I gave birth to with Dr Pastor Ian Thurlby Campbell, I will always love all of you, thank you God loves you, God bless you.

CHAPTER 1 - WINSTON gave excellent speech why criminologist place crime over social harm IN ADDITION LAW ON JURISPRUDENCE / THEORY IN LEGAL RESEARCH, CRIMINOLOGY, CONTRACT, CRIMINAL LAW, CONSTITUTIONAL / PUBLIC LAW, LAW SKILLS / LEGAL SKILLS AND SYSTEMS, LEGAL SKILLS AND METHODS, TORT, EQUITY AND TRUST, EVIDENCE, EU LAW.

- Grange Hill For Girls , Part 2: Exams and all that manly jazz for ladies! LOOKING AT THEME TELEVISION CULTURE IS HOW WE SHOULD BEHAVE CONDUCT OWES THEME LITERATURE OWES THANKSGIVING MORAL

- lactulose
- Gaviscone

- Ivory Coast ; Corporate Crimes of the Suite.

//....//

CHAPTER 2 - RAYCHELLIE took economics4makeup class to learn more about market structure of monopoly market and perfect competition competitive market tutorials IN ADDITION - fdd202 - TMA01 Demand Curve, Minimum Efficient Scale M.E.S. sa3aug16 - fdd202 - TMA02 game theory,monopoly,competition saaug16 - fdd202 - TMA03 labor Supply&Demand, income distribution-tues27may08 - fdd202 - TMA04 AD, stock market wealth, accelerator model - fdd202 - TMA05 int'l trade, int'l finance - fdd202 – TMA06 – MACROECONOMIC Inflation, Economic Growth, fdd202 - TMA06 inflat, interest rate, investment unemployment.

LORENZ CURVE, GINI COEFFICIENT, MEAN, STANDARD DEVIATION.

//....//

PART A – RESEARCH METHODS, LAW

PART B – MATHS, SCIENCE PROJECT EXAMPLES

PART B – eBUSINESS PROJECT REPORT EXAMPLE, MONOPOLY MARKET AND COMPETITIVE ENTRY EXPLAINED - SEMIOTICS, TEXTUAL ANALYSIS - BELL/CASTELLS 'INFORMATION SOCIETY' ON 'WORK'- MEDIA POLICY, SOCIAL JUSTICE SOCIAL POLICY, CRIME AND JUSTICE, CRIMINOLOGY, EBUSINESS ECONOMICS

//...//

PART A

- Validity (the degree to which the research study results supports the intended conclusion.
- Reliability (the idea that under specific conditions, the research study results fits the time and purpose for which it was designed
- .Comprehensiveness (the research study results shows connections among issues e.g.social services, education and training, economic development and housing
- Coherence (the requirement for the research study results to 'fit' pre-exisiting believes

LAW, WHAT IS LAW, CONTROLLING BEHAVIOURS, CREATING FAIRNESS FREEDOMS, INDIVIDUAL AND THE STATE, CASE LAW CREATED BY JUDGES, ACTS OF PARLIAMENT / LEGISLATION CREATED BY GOVERNMENT, COURTS OF HUMAN RIGHTS ANOTHER BODY OF LAW, TORT LAW CORRECTING WRONGFUL ACT THROUGH COMPENSATION PERSONAL INJURY INSURANCE, RULE OF LAW AV DICEY.

PART B

MATHS – SIMULTANEOUS EQUATIONS, SCIENCE <u>INVESTIGATION: RATE OF REACTION</u>

PART C

POLICY AND THE SOCIAL SCIENCES AND LITERATURE

MEDIA POLICY

TEXTUAL ANALYSIS – DENOTATION, CONNOTATION, SIGNIFIER, SIGNIFIED, SEMIOTICS

BELL / CASTELLS 'INFORMATION SOCIETY' ON 'WORK' Outline Bell's and Castells' research on the 'information society'. What would you need to consider in evaluating their research? Answer 'Work'

SOCIAL JUSTICE, CRIME JUSTICE, SOCIAL POLICY, CRIMINOLOGY

ECONOMICS - PARETO EFFICIENT MARKET IS COMPETITVE MARKET ,

- ASSYMETRIC INFORMATION AND HOW YOU SORT 'LEMON' CAR INFORMATION, STARTING POINT ALL SECOND HAND CARS ARE LEMON
- ENGLISH LITERATURE

CARS NO WAY OF TELLING CAR WORKS UNLESS TAKE IT HOME AND TEST IT OUT - PROJECT **Topic Title: Determinants of Wage Biases in the UK Labour Market**

CONTENTS PAGE

10 – REFERENCES AND KEY SOURCES AND RESOURCES

11 - APPENDICES
    APPENDIX 1: TABLE OF RESULTS
    APPENDIX 2: SYMBOLS USED

For the Purposes of the Quantitative Analysis Project regarding Wage Discrimination and Wage Differentials, during my period at Residential School at the University of Bath, I obtained a set of Econometric Results. Econometrics is the application of statistics to study economic data, in this case Wage Discrimination and Wage Differentials. The Econometric Results was obtained using Dummy Variables (where Dummy Variables in a regression model have two categories, valued zero and 1, where e.g. male = 0 and female = 1). The Econometric Results is also based on the Ordinary Least Square (OLS) Linear Regression which is a technique used for estimating the unknown parameters (relationship between e.g. dependent γ Variable Wages and independent χ Variable Region etc) in a linear regression model by employing formals such as adjusted R squared (R^2) and P-Value etc. My Econometric Results uses Multiple Regression (defined below) for the basis of looking at number of casual factors (independent χ Variables) such as Employment, being Female etc., to test for any relationship with the dependent γ Variable Wages, in order to find any evidence to support the Alternative Hypothesis of Wage Differentials or in the extreme case, if the strength of relationship is strong enough between the dependent γ Variable, and multiple χ Variables, suggesting evidence for the Null Hypothesis that Wage Discrimination may exist.

/....................../

CHAPTER 1 - WINSTON gave excellent speech why criminologist place crime over social harm IN ADDITION LAW ON JURISPRUDENCE / THEORY IN LEGAL RESEARCH, CRIMINOLOGY, CONTRACT, CRIMINAL LAW, CONSTITUTIONAL / PUBLIC LAW, LAW SKILLS / LEGAL SKILLS AND SYSTEMS, LEGAL SKILLS AND METHODS, TORT, EQUITY AND TRUST, EVIDENCE, EU LAW.

- Grange Hill For Girls , Part 2: Exams and all that manly jazz for ladies! LOOKING AT THEME TELEVISION CULTURE IS HOW WE SHOULD BEHAVE CONDUCT OWES THEME LITERATURE OWES THANKSGIVING MORAL

- lactulose
- Gaviscone

- Ivory Coast ; Corporate Crimes of the Suite.

//

Tithe , offering is to GROW CHURCH is God well pleased investing in things of God is creating heirs , will surely be blessed MALACHI 3:10.

//

JURISPRUDENCE -LAW OF LEGAL POSITIVISM see John Austin, Hans Kelsen, HLA Hart – LEGAL POSITIVISM (SOCIAL CONSTRUCT created by human acts and social institutions eg POLITICS), RELIGION (God - natural law), MORALITY (INFLUENCE OR ALTER CONDUCT/BEHAVIOUR), In response to av dicey's equality before rule of law / rule / law that power groups have unfair advantage over weaker groups that mental health social service criminal justice system police court psychology psychiatry practitioners assume themselves arbitrary powers to force psychotic injection (I HAVE BEEN ADMINISTERED HADOL HALDOT DEPO, PARIPALIDONE, RESPIRIDONE, ZUCLOTHENTIXOE DECANOATE CLOPIXOL, ARIPRIPRAZOL, DIPOXOL) that causes (social) harm disability sickness (GENERAL PRACTITIONER (GP) DIAGNOSIS – SALBUTAMOL VENTOLIN EVOHALER INHALER FOR ASTHMA, FERROUS SULPHATE IRON FOLIC ACID FOR THALASSEMIA, INSULIN LEVEMIR FOR DIABETES, LEUKEMIA) on law abiding service users
: Esther says Mordecai - u look down on the Jews bcos u are Queen Esther of Susa, Persia (Iran), If u keep silent of Haman plan slaughter Jews in Gallows, Deliverance will come from somewhere (for the people of God) and Esther u will surely perish.
//
ECONOMIC DEVELOPMENT Wiki Quality of Life QoL is well being of individuals and societies, outlining negative and positive features of life e.g. physical health, family, education , employment, wealth, religious beliefs, finance and the environment.

/

Mid Year 2008 President George W Bush announced to wage war in Nigeria. Boko Haram were two-fold in their struggle and aim to forbid western education/media, this destroyed war.

Communist Germany and West Germany pioneers to lead way TV broadcasting so raced communist propaganda ahead of other nations this influenced war.

LAW of MOSES mosaic MOSIAC LAW - Israelites were enslaved 500 years in EGYPT AFRICA by PHARAOH after death their HEIR JOSEPH ISRAELITE GORVENOR OF EGYPT WHO LEAD THEM THERE TO THEIR FIRST LAND. ISRAELITE MOSES FAIR COMPLEXION TO PHARAOH defeated PHARAOH hence the LAW OF MOSES (EYE FOR EYE CUT IT OFF, COURT) favour fairer skin over dark skin. JESUS NEIGHBOUR PRINCIPLE TURN OTHER CHEEK DUTY OF CARE GOOD SAMARITAN SETTLE DISPUTE OUT OF COURT IS JUSTICE FAIRNESS CHANGE.

/

Song of Pharaoh Africa

Chorus
Lord of Pharaoh Africa song; Lord of praise and worship sound;
Lord of the dance string wind percussion King David psalm;
God almighty How Great you are one; My beautiful one My beautiful one; God almighty How Great you are one.

/verse 1
God of ancient of days... Lord of thy day thy dawn;
Moses wilderness son.. of man be lifted Apostle Paul bless thy tongue;
Pharaoh Africa arise.... we plead the Lord we're one;
/verse 2
Pharaoh Africa praise.... our forgiveness under grace ;
Christ sovereign Lion... of Judah thy countenance;
Lamb thy Cross of Mosaic... Moses under Law took our place;

//
Dedicated to Dr. Pastor Ian Thurlby Campbell (18 August 1980), there will be always no other i love this guy like no other, i love and u will always be my true one, i love the work you do for the church, incl. prayer training, so loving and peaceful, would like more children Gods heirs, i love you i love my quiet time love God, i put him first without the Lord's loving mercy there will be no us, our kids, the Grace of our Lord Jesus Christ thru disparity endured under the Law of Moses society world Romans chapter 8 ,

and dedicated to our children in your care Dr Pastor Ian Thurlby Campbell,

our daughter Rachel Katie Christie Adeniji Dr Pastor Ian Thurlby Campbell in care
snatched in knife violence neighbour Jean 48 Albert Westcott House , Alberta Street
SE17 3SE neighbour fatality,

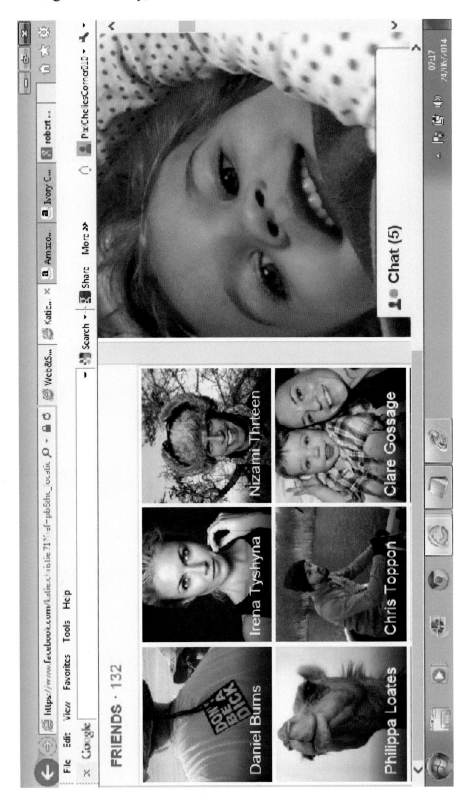

our sixtuplets/quintuplets? sons born January 2006 KCA office in care of Keith Carter, Keith Carter and Associates KCA , 142 Liverpool Road N1 1LA, our son , Dr Pastor Ian Thurlby Campbell, in care of Robert Harland, Richard Harland Maudsley Hospital Denmark Hill SE5 8AZ, Mummy hasn't forgotten all of you, God hasn't forgotten all of you In Jesus' Name Amen x Love Mummy, Rachel Adeniji xx

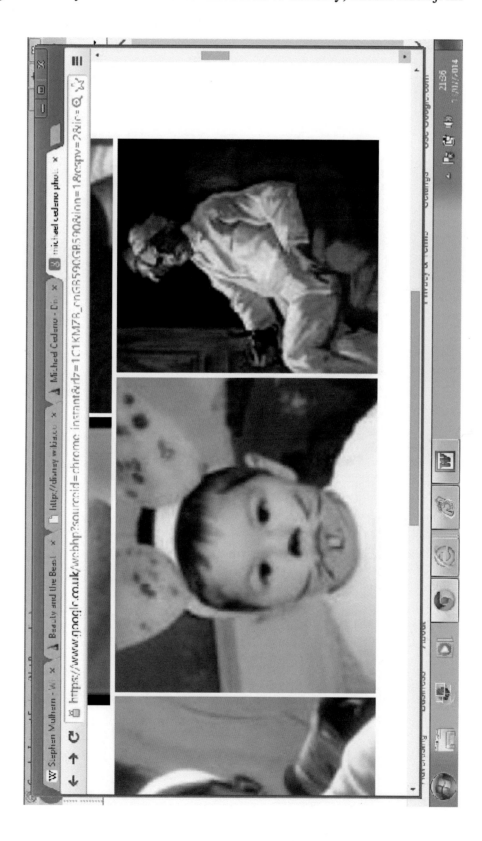

WINSTON gave excellent speech why criminologist place crime over social harm, RAYCHELLIE took economics4makeup class to learn more about market structure of monopoly market and perfect competition competitive market tutorials.

Winston&Chellie, things don't always go, turned out as plan, but one thing is certain Raychellie thought 'the bible tells us that Faith is the substance of things hoped for and the evidence of things not yet seen, that everything works for good God's plan to those that are called according to God's purpose.

"So what makes you such a brilliant Solicitor thats good at their job" Raychellie asks, "Its knowing that God is the only natural leader", replies Winston, "Politicians say parliament house of commons is split down the middle, the bible also says that satan is divided such a kingdom cannot stand".

Song playing,i have had my share of ups and down, if anyone ever writes my life story, your the best thing that ever happened to me.

WINSTON thought about helping RAYCHELLIE with a COURT ORDER banning her EX-PARTNER Sacha Singh Rooprai from coming near her on the evidence that he pushed RAYCHELLIE over an 11th floor storey balcony and his new wife SERKAN groped RAYCHELLIE nd new infant son urinated SPECIMEN on RAYCHELLIE.
/
bigger tales , d blacker , diary 4 single black female.
Raychellie 28 year old entrepeuner studying biochemistry for cosmetic make-up, had just met Winston Churchill, 30 years old an Solicitor, a Jamaican Caribbean, Jamo boy, nigerians would call it, Raychellie Adeniyi had just met Winston Churchill that evening at a speed dating event on a yacht on the River Thames Westminster Bridge Road. The twist to the event was Star Sign centred, all the star signs were grouped into elements Air, Earth, Fire, Water. Thats how Raychellie and Winston Churchill had met and got acquainted to one and other, from this Raychellie and Winston had a natural desire of love in their eyes and affection when they clocked each other from different angles across the room lounge onboard the speed dating love boat.
Bradley Wyatt Chiquitita from the Netherlands and had grown up in the States was the first to approach Raychellie, they had just five minutes a pencil and a paper to jot down preferences and whether
would like to meet again. Within few minutes gone by, Winston had moved to Raychellie's table. Being the only black background in the room and quite touching and moved about each other s expectation of the other, they both felt relieved to be by each other. " Hello darling, Winston Churchill" is my name I am a Leo, how but you?".
"Hi" replied Raychellie, "I am Raychellie, I am Aries".
"Nice name" replied Winston "So how did the name come about?"
"From two names Rachel and Shelly". "How about you?" Smiled Raychellie Winston Churchill are you acquaintainted with Churchill?" "My grandfather's Regimen
Event lasted 7-9pm but stayed locally at the Federal Bar for some cocktail drinks Pina Colada and Bloody Mary. Winston was handsome and career settled, Raychellie

thought, and that she could match that, she was equally beautiful as he with a shimmer of tahitian glow bronze tan to her skin complexion and wavy frizzy bronze hair. Equally Winston was pale complexion with frizzy black hair, she studied perused this guy as he sat legs spread apart threw the napkin on the table smiled head down and stroked his moustache. "So Chellie, what would you want from me as a man out of life i like you very much".

song have you ever, reached out for the other side, i may be climbing on rainbow (played).

The mood was appropriate for this guys lips to take manly SERAPHIM charge of her CHERUBIM lady feminity a damsel to be rescued.

Raychellie reach over and hugged his six pack, and said , "I have a confession to make, I am Nigerian, sorry! Baby how do you feel, talk? Are you disappointed?"

"Of course, i am disappointed" replies Winston, what can i say, nigerians sold us into slavery, nigerians i seen are light skin with picky hair, but girl you are so fine damn fine what can I say, Chellie girl from next door, a neighbourly one, or Chellie from the block the United States Americans would call it, this is a difficult situation for me, i need time", he gets ups and excuses himself for fresh air.

/
WHY CRIMINOLOGIST PLACE CRIME OVER SOCIAL HARM? ANSWER Criminology old bailey press isbn 1858364922 michael doherty CRIMINOLOGY is the STUDY of CRIME created by law is PUNISHABLE (SOCIAL CONSTRUCT) not all SOCIAL HARM is CRIME. Criminology study of criminal behavior,causes of crime and also the origins of criminal laws, process of law enforcement crown prosecution service CPS and social reaction effects to crime/deviance.

Wiki in Social Deviance /What is Crime and Deviance defines SOCIAL HARM as 'the level of harm that a particular crime puts on society' For instance the level of harm that a crime harms only the criminal is low because there are no harm/social harm done to the victim/victimless. Also the level of harm that crime hurts others or social institution such as harm in the work place is considered high eg DEATH chinese cockle pickers (film 'Ghosts) & CORPORATE CRIME (work place practices, fraud, environmental pollution, insider trading, tax evasion, white collar crime) cause more monetary damage than small-time theft, but SOCIAL RESPONSE IS MINIMAL. Drug usage considered low in social harm, while whereas an act such as serial murder considered high social harm.

Isbn 9780199290543 oxford companion to law p282 defines criminological research as the study/research into criminal behaviour and the cause(s) of crime that classical school early approach Cesare Beccaria, Jeremy Bentham etc assumedthat offenders were RATIONAL PERSONS who have chosen to break the law for their own advantage (criminal behaviour). In the twentieth century Sociology 'the theory of anomie' and 'strain' proposed by Emile Durkheim, Robert Merton and others etc., explored the extent to which crime is the product of the push by all individuals for personal success, and the fustrations of those who lack the LIFE OPPORTUNITIES to achieve those goals legitimately.

E.g. Whiterose shopping centre at edge of Leeds UK socially excludes youth of five or more in hoodies (LABELLING) and the poor not because they are criminal but because the cant afford to shop there. Social exclusion because of being poor lack of skills education are (CAUSES OF CRIME). LABELLING THEORY developed by Howard Becker and others research into offending behaviours AND the manner in which society reacts to it, STIGMATIZING INDIVIDUALS AND GROUPS, AND OFTEN PERPETUATING CRIMINAL LIFE-STYLES. E.g. MINORITY GROUPS e.g. Poor , blacks. CRIMINAL JUSTICE SYSTEM afro caribbean greatly over-represented in PRISON.

//
LEGAL SYSTEMS AND METHODS:

WWW.lawnerds.com/guide/irac.HTML

THE IRAC FORMULA is Issue spotting, Rule e.g duty of care, duress, Analysis whether the facts fit the rule, Conclusion whether the RULE apply to the facts.

IRAC (Issue, rule (rule or rule of law or the law e.g neighbour principle / duty of care owed by manufacturer of ginger beer in the case Donoghue v Stevenson (1932)), Analysis & Conclusion).

Learning Legal Rules: James Holland and Julian Webb

p113 IRAC formula - Issue spotting , Rule, Analysis - compare 'facts' to the 'rule' to form the analysis, Conclusion from analysis conclude yes or no whether RULE applies to FACTS conclude with OBITER OPINION.

/
JUDICIAL CREATIVITY IN DOCTRINE OF JUDICIAL PRECEDENT :

Richard Wortley
p355

STARE DECISIS means 'to stand by what has been decided' and in STARE DECISIS past COMMON LAW (is also known as PRECEDENT/CASE LAW) and STARE DECISIS is the body of PAST common law that binds JUDGES that make future decisions to ensure consistent treatment. STARE DECISIS is the basis of JUDICIAL PRECEDENT;

RATIO DECIDENDI means 'the reason for deciding' .The legal principle of past cases must be followed in FUTURE cases of SIMILAR fact by the same and all courts below it. RATIO DECIDENDI - this is a BINDING PRECEDENT for future cases where the facts are similar decided in a senior court or same level court; the RATIO DECIDENDI of R v Howe (1987) is that 'duress' is no defence to murder by making ' DURESS' opinion OBITER. In the judgement the Judge may discuss not only the RATIO DECIDENDI but other matters e.g. OBITER ODICTA OPINION. The RATIO DECIDENDI of the case Brown (1993), that the defendants were found 'guilty' of offences under the ss47 and s20 of the offences Against the Person Act

1861 (past legislation binding future cases), because the defence of consent which had pleaded to respect of their sado-masochistic practices at a private party, was not available to defendants charged with such an offence. The House of Lord expressed the OBITER opinion that consent was a DEFENCE in other circumstances such as ritual circumcision tattooing ear & body piercing & violent sports.

OBITER DICTA / OBITER DICTUM means' things said by the way' or 'other things said' may influence judges in later cases as PERSUASIVE PRECEDENT. Bowen LJ in Carlill v Carbolic Smoke Ball Co. (1892) where Smoke Ball company said impossible to make offer to whole world therefore no contract, Bowen LJ - 'persuasive precedent' - obiter that if an advert / ad is posed to the world to find a dog for a reward, it is a contract ;

Gary Slapper & David Kelly
/

IF HOWEVER, THE COURT FINDS THAT THE CURRENT DISPUTE (Case brought to court by Claimant/ Plaintiff against Defendant e.g Donoghue v / against Stevenson (1932) where manufacturer Stevenson in neighbour principle - a judicial precedent, owed a 'duty of care' to Mrs Donoghue who fell violently ill emptying a decomposed snail from the opaque glass of her ginger beer) IS FUNDAMENTALLY DISTANT FROM ALL PREVIOUS CASES CALLED A 'MATTER OF IMPRESSION', Judges have the authority and duty to make law by creating PRECEDENT (CASE LAW).

The creative role of Judges - The relationship between parliament and judiciary - according to the unwritten constitution, Parliament is responsible for making law, and judges for interpreting and applying the law.

/
CREATIVITY within STATUTORY INTERPRETATION.

STATUTORY INTERPRETATION is Judges are assisted by certain 'RULES' AND PRESUMPTION in the interpretation of ACT OF PARLIAMENT (also known as STATUTES or LEGISLATION or ACT eg Employment Act drafted by Parliamentary counsel called drafsmen).
In STATUTORY INTERPRETATION, the RULES OF INTERPRETATION are LITERAL RULE GOLDEN RULE, MISCHIEF RULE.

//
Isbn9781408519714, p300 COMMON LAW crime is elements defined in case law rather than by statute
#Common Injury: A public nuisance is one that affects a right, a protection or a benefit enjoyed in common by members of the affected class. obstruction of a road is a public nuisance it interferes with the public's ability to make use of a right of way. Eg Lyons, Sons & Co. V Gulliver (1913) the defendant committed a public nuisance regularly allowed large queues4cheap seats to build up on the pavement outside his theatre, impeding access to the claimant's shop.
A case of public nuisance can reach the courts in three ways: Public nuisance is a
*common law crime, and will be investigated by the police and prosecuted by the

Crown Prosecution Service CPS like any other offence. Secondly, if a criminal case is not sufficient to deal with the problem , then the Attorney General has the power (but not the duty) to seek an injunction in the civil courts on behalf of the public
Third third route into
the courts is a civil action brought by an individual who show that he has suffered a special or particular damage ie a loss or injury over and above the rest of the members of the class. In Tate & Lyle Industies v Greater London Council (1983) the defendant caused a public nuisance by causing a river to become silted, thus interfering with public navigation rights. The claimant suffered special loss as it had to pay for dredging works to allow ships to reach its jetty
p102 THE RELATIONSHIP BETWEEN *COMMON LAW and STATUTORY ASPECTS OF THE LAW
*IN relation to the terms of a CONTRACT, you should understand and apply the common law rules and the statutory rules and how both aspects relate.
E.g.*EXPRESSED TERMS (are agreed)
*IMPLIED TERMS (created by STATUTE / LAW)
Two ways in which the *Common law may imply a term into a contract
p99 1)The Moorcock(1889) -'business efficacy' 'official bystander' tests,2)Terms implied by custom eg HuttonvWarren1836
#2ways statute implies a term into a contract. (Terms implied by) 1)Sale of

 Goods Act 1979,2)Supply of Goods&ServicesAct1977
#one way *common law may *prohibit a contract term, p100 Term not in Contract
#two ways *statute may *prohibit a contract term eg 1)Unfair Contracts Term Act 1977,2)Unfair Terms in Consumer Contracts Regulat1999
#common law is not *limited to the type of term to be implied ie *Moorcock & Hutton v Warren cases, terms were implied into d respective contracts to cover the 'safety' f d mooring n d 'loss of profit' leavin tenanted land.
#Statute is limited as to the type of term to be implied. Ie the statutes imply terms as the quality of goods when sold or transfered and/or the standard of services supplied and the time for completion of the contract.
#Common law may exclude any type of term from a contract if the requirement of a point is not followed.
#Statute is limited to prohibiting exclusion and/or limitation terms (absolutely or allowing the term if reasonable) or, in consumer contracts only , prohibiting any type of term if 'unfair'.

//
Isbn9780748798650 p77 The legal system - The civil courts and other forms of dispute resolution
-EQUITY - a branch of law which developed from the end of the 13th century. It is based on the court's application of 'FAIRNESs' to a decision in a case , in response to the occassional unfairness of the inflexible rules of *COMMON LAW.

#OUTLINE OF CIVIL COURTS AND APPEAL SYSTEM

County Court > High Court > Court of Appeal > House of Lords

#MAGISTRATES' COURT is primarily a criminal court but does have some *CIVIL JURISDICTION over family matters (except divorce). It can deal with recovery of

unpaid council tax and charges for water, gas and electricity, it can hear local authority appeals re whether to grant licences for gambling or the sale of alcohol.
#COUNTY COURT deals with many cases on civil disputes including cases on contract, tort (eg negligence), bankruptcy, property and divorce cases.
Civil cases are divided into 3 types 1) cases less than £5,000 are transferred to SMALL CLAIMS

TRACK and are dealt with and heard by DISTRICT JUDGE. 2) cases between £5,000 AND £15,000 transferred to the FAST TRACK and generally heard by CIRCUIT JUDGE, 3)cases over £15,000 are usually tranferred to the MULTI-TRACK and may be heard by CIRCUIT JUDGE or may be transferred to the HIGH COURT.

#HIGH COURT has 3 divisions:
1) QUEEN'S BENCH DIVISION main court and deals with primarily contract and tort cases. Approx. 70 High Court Judges sitting in this court. Cases are often heard at ROYAL COURTS OF JUSTICE in THE STRAND, LONDON or heard at HIGH COURT'S DISTRICT REGISTRIES around the country.
2) FAMILY DIVISION dealing family matters including divorce, related children and finincial claims, adoption and care proceedings.

3) CHANCERY DIVISION : Historically dealt with cases in which the rules of EQUITY could be used. The modern version of this court deals with cases such as partnership disputes, company law, disputes re wills, trusts, bankruptcy, the sale of land and the creation of mortgages.Heard
at ROYAl COURTS OF JUSTICEor CHANCERY CENTRES
/
auction sales p17, an auctioneer's call for bids is an INVITATION TO TREAT, bids placed by person are OFFERs which auctioneer can accept or reject as he chooses, obligation s: contract law d.g. cracknell, old bailey press isbn 1858365023, also revision book. see precedent case common law (administrative judge law) case Payne v (against) Cave (1789), this principle of INVITATION TO TREAT and OFFER has a statute statutory legislative (parliament legislation) form in s57(2) Sale of Goods ACT 1979 which a sale by auction is completed by the fall of the hammer and, up until then, a lot can be withdrawn by auctioneer before he accepts the bid.

/
p12 constitutional law isbn 1858364604

CONSTITUTIONAL CONVENTIONS = behaviour of government eg queen in parliament, state opening of parliament.

/
UNWRITTEN CONSTITUTION means PARLIAMENTARY SOVEREIGNTY , parliament is sovereign supreme power ruler and can make and unmake law. a.v. dicey said a WRITTEN CONSTITUTION eg a BILL OF RIGHTS would bind parliament law-making powers would bind on old law when making future laws.

a.v. dicey unwritten constitution everyone equal before the law however seen power groups having unfair advantage over weaker groups poor working class miners forced to strike by power union and miners lost job in failure of mines strike which forced thatcher to enforce RULE OF LAW that no-one is above the law and is equal before the law.

/

CONSTITUTIONAL PRINCIPLES are SEPARATION OF POWERS / BALANCE OF POWER between 1) LEGISLATIVE Parliament Legislature ; 2) EXECUTIVE cabinet , and 3) JUDICIAL Judge ; to avoid autocratic and tyrannical government.

DEMOCRACY IS ACCOUNTABLE GOVERNMENT TO ELECTORATE/VOTER.

CONSTITUTIONAL PRINCIPLES IS ALSO SOVEREIGNTY OF PARLIAMENT.

/

lactulose
Gaviscone
/

Ivory Coast ; Corporate Crimes of the Suite. Sacha Singh Rooprai came back ten years later, with Serkan his partner & infant son & MENTAL HEALTH ACT MHA POLICE PUT GUN TO MY HEAD, CUT MY HAIR SECTIONED ME for no reason at my Ivory's Address 46 Albert Westcott House , Alberta Street, London , United Kingdom SE17 3SE. Serkan's gran Jean next door at 48 Albert Westcott House, Alberta Street, London United Kingdom SE17 3SE, ST GILES SE5 7UD & SLAM MAUDSLEY SE5 8AZ & COUNCIL & CAMELOT SCHOOL SE15 1QP & MS JENNY YO, HEARTBEAT SE5 7NL , SACHA SINGH ROOPRAI & HIS INFANT SON with KELLY SERKAN & MHA POLICE GROPED, BEAT, KNIFED & URINATED specimen over Ivory's body & face, the police officer on Ivory's case could give no other good reason than Ivory had committed fraud by having a publishing contract which Ivory had used to further her faith & studies, Ivory's home was bugged with electronic spy smoke alarms the council had fitted early summer June that year 2014 before the first tuesday in December the Incident had happen and enjoyed praising God to premier
christian radio. This day, the speaker on Ivory spy camera smoke alarm had spoken, it was Maria Tott Rodriguez who had screamed requested in from Premier Christian Radio station in Victoria Embankment London SW1 for Ivory Coast's Premier Christian Radio freeview TV to be "turned off" not to evolve themselves in Ivory Coast. Ivory was mocked with a crown of torns twice and Ivory screamed "take it off it hurts" each time. First Thurs December 2015 Ivory stop' listenin Premier 4 TBN station she create from publishin sectioned same officer

//

Grange Hill For Girls , Part 2: Exams and all that manly jazz for ladies!

John Dickson inaugurate cover for the supply teacher Jim Birley short for James. It was before the literature exam. "Literature is very important it is part of English modern classic, culture that tells us how we should BEHAVE / CONDUCT, it is part of television culture, THEME we learn from LITERATURE whether society agrees with it enough to form a value a politics a policy stand a modern day Pharissees and Saducees policy document helping Christ and Apostles debate the defiled , sinners into the Kingdom of Heaven, so literature owes thanks giving, okay, Theme Inspector Calls by JBPriestly Says Capitalism fragments society v help we're one body. Rachel Adeniji are happy to see me.

No looking for Lavande Corpse, Kingsley, Seun Adeniyi outside the school gates, focus on your exams for the time being.
//
* Statute is legislation is Acts of parliament e.g. Employment Act 1998 , Crime and Disorder Act 1998 and is drafted by parliamentary counsel (draftsmen).
* Common law is precedent is case law e.g. Donoghue v Stevenson (1932) , Donoghue v (against) Stevenson.
- role of parliament to create law
- role of judges to apply the law

old bailey press : p4 criminal law revision workbook isbn 1858364612 ; pp8-9 evidence revision workbook isbn 1858363845 .

Question : K attacked J's young son. J later saw K suffering epileptic fit near a puddle. J did nothing and watch K drown. Advise J of his CRIMINAL LIABILITY.

If Any LIABILITY on failing to act and killing by GROSS NEGLIGENCE. Issues on CAUSATION also arise. Question asks J LIABILITY so DO NOT be tempted to discuss K. K dies making his liability academic.

peter darwent, Ian yule, pub. philip allan , aqa law as unit 2 , ISBN 978-1-4441-7157-0, www.philipallan.co.uk/studentunitguides.

ROBBERY - the action to rob a person or place by force (violent offences).

THEFT ACT 1968 - the action or crime of stealing or dishonestly appropriating property from the other to permanently deprive the other.

BURDEN OF PROOF - defendant to prove not guilty eg shooting was accident or D pushed E rival gang from 3 storeys to teach lesson only, law consider danger.

AIDING & ABETTING - aider&abetter -person present assisting or encouraging at the scene of the offence.

AUTOMATISM - accused defendant is not controlling or aware of their ACTIONS. COURTS distinguish action that endanger others & those that pose no threat.

CRIMES OF OMISSION. OMISSION - failure to act. FIVE AREAS where such liability for omission exists. 1) DUTY ARISING FROM A CONTRACT (CASE COMMON LAW PRECEDENT), this occurs when failure to perform a contractual obligation endangers life. see R v (against) Pittwood (1902) or R v Pittwood (1902). - 2) Duty arising from STATUTE (ACTS OF PARLIAMENT LEGISLATION), see Children and Young Persons Act 1933 where the ACT / ACTION / CONDUCT results failure to provide a child medical care. see Road Traffic ACT 1988 where failure to wear a seat belt or failure to stop and report a road accident. - 3) VOLUNTARY ASSUMPTION OF A DUTY where someone voluntarily takes responsibility for another person or assumes the positive duty to act for the general welfare of that person. see R v Stone and Dobinson (1977) where an unmarried cohabiting couple invited Stone's middle-age sister who is anorexic, to live with them. the sister later died from her health neglecting herself which Stone and Dobinson were aware. Stone and Dobinson were convicted of her manslaughter, they had assumed a duty of care of her, a duty that they could easily have discharged by calling for help or providing even basic care. - 4) DUTY ARISING FROM PRIOR CONDUCT, where if the defendant accidentally commits an act that causes harm, and subsequently becomes aware of the danger he or she has created, there arises a duty to act reasonably to avert that danger. see R v Miller (1983). Lord Diplock had no doubt that the defendant had been convicted correctly for the actus reus of the offence of arson is present if the defendant accidentally starts a fire and fails to take steps to extinguish it or prevent damage due to an intention to destroy or damage property belonging to another or being reckless whether any such property destroyed or damaged. - 5) PUBLIC DUTY , A person in a public office may be under a duty to care for others e.g. Carer , Doctor or Family Doctor , Police Officer. see R v Dytham (1979), a police officer was held to be guilty of a crime when, without justification, he failed to perform his duty to preserve the Queen's Peace by not protecting a citizen who was being kicked to death.

LIABILITY / CRIMINAL LIABILITY - that is, liability to be prosecuted in a criminal court and, if convicted, to be punished by the STATE - is an ACTUS REUS (guilty action - the physical element e.g. beating someone unconscious) accompanied by the appropriate MENS REA (guilty mind - the mental element eg after beating someone unconscious throwing them in a river lake to drown them with intent guilty more and of killing them).

INTENTION - offender makes a decision to break the law.

MISTAKE - failure to foresee a consequence and MISTAKE in the sense of lack of knowledge of surrounding circumstance and are treated differently in law.

DEFINE RECKLESSNESS - is where an offender acts (takes action) while realising that there is possibility that his or her action could cause the illegal action.

DEFINE GROSS NEGLIGENCE means the defendant did not forsee causing harm, but should have realised the risks involved. An example the s R v Adomako (1995), where an anaesthetist failed to notice for 6 minutes that an oxygen tube had become disconnected from the ventilator. By this time, the patient had suffered a cardiac arrest and attempts to resuscitate were unsuccessful.

NON-FATAL OFFENCES - EXCEPT s.18 wounding or causing grievous bodily harm with INTENT, and with UNLAWFUL KILLING - MURDER. NON-FATAL can be committed either intentionally or recklessly e.g. D attacked E, E sustained graze (non-fatal) courts have no power to enforce law for non-fatal.

VOLUNTARY MANSLAUGHTER - loss of self control (INTOXICATION / DRUNK), dimished responsibility (MENTAL ILL) s.2 Homicide Act 1957.

INVOLUNTARY MANSLAUGHTER - unlawful killing without malice aforethought, breach duty of care, gross negligence.

CAUSATION - this occurs in so-called RESULT CRIMES - which is those where the defendant's actions cause the prohibited result. In murder, for example, the prosecution must prove a CAUSAL LINK BETWEEN THE DEFENDANT'S ACTION AND THE DEATH OF THE VICTIM.

FACTUAL CAUSATION / FACTUAL RULE OF CAUSATION - is referred to as 'BUT FOR' TEST requires the prosecution to prove that 'BUT FOR' THE DEFENDANT'S ACT, THE HARM WILL NOT HAVE OCCURRED. See case / common law / precedent R v White (1910), where the defendant put potassium cyanide into a drink with INTENT to murder his mother. The medical evidence showed that she died not of poisoning but of heart failure. The defendant was acquitted of murder and convicted of attempted murder.

LEGAL RULE OF CAUSATION - means there must be something that could reasonably been FORESEEN as a consequence of the unlawful act e.g. the defendant contributed 'significant contribution', to the act and 'operative and substantial cause of harm'. see a.m. dugdale in a level law pub. Butterworths 1996, - A points a gun at B and B dies of a heart attack. - A knocks B unconscious and leaves him lying in a road, where he is run over by a car and killed. - A injures B, who is being taken by ambulance to the hospital. The ambulance crashes, killing all the occupants. - A knocks B unconscious and she remains lying in a street for several hours, where she is robbed, raped or assaulted further. - A (AIDER & ABETTER) CAUSED THE CONSEQUENCE , ON THE BASIS OF THAT NONE OF THESE EVENTS WOULD HAVE HAPPENED ' BUT FOR' THE INITIAL ATTACK BY A ON B. - The difficulty with this approach is it can LINK AN INITIAL CAUSE (the attack) with consequences that are both highly IMPROBABLE and UNFORESEEABLE. this has been a problem for unlawful killing - murder and manslaughter - where there is a less direct link between ACT and EFFECT. IN SUCH CASES, ONE HAS TO CONSIDER THE RESPONSIBILITY OF THE DEFENDANT FOR THE VICTIM'S DEATH. see R v Marjoram (1999) ; R v Cheshire (1991) ; R v Smith (1959).

LIABILITY for OMISSION - OMISSION being failure to act - any DUTY arising from failure to act , watching someone dying.

PRINCIPLE OF LIABILITY FOR FAILING TO ACT - A GOOD SAMARITAN LAW.

ALTERNATIVELY base LIABILITY on a positive act - consider chain of CAUSATION in fact and in law.

types of homicide - KILLING BY GROSS NEGLIGENCE.

LOOK AT BOTH SIDES E.G. J LIABILITY AND DOES J HAVE ANY DEFENCES E.G. J's SON ATTACKED BY K. ANXIETY IS NOT ENOUGH, CONSIDER J's DEFENCE OF OTHERS E.G. J's SON ATTACKED BY K.

DUTY TO ACT can arise under STATUTE (ACTS OF PARLIAMENT LEGISLATION) e.g. Children and Young Persons ACT 1933 or under CONTRACT (CASE LAW COMMON LAW PRECEDENT) see R v Pittwood (1902) 19 TLR 34.

Neither Children & Young Persons Act 1933 and R v Pittwood (1902) 19 TLR 34, could form basis legal duty resting on J given facts.

no evidence of any NOVUS ACTUS INTERVENIENS.

COMMON LAW,DUTY TO ACT can arise if the defendant J is a BLOOD RELATIVE of the victim K, see R v Instan (1893) 1QB 450 or if SPECIAL RELATIONSHIP between parties e.g. Carer or Doctor or Police Officer, see R v Stone and Dobinson (1977) QB 354, e.g. if J was caring for K.

QUESTION -Advise J of his CRIMINAL LIABILITY if any would make if J had driven slowly to a point at which an ambulance was coming delayed the ambulance arrival to scene of accident.
ANSWER- public nuisance only, need evidence or confession for crime.

//

Winston & Chellie ; The Bachelor of Law, Economics thu1sep16
WINSTON AND CONTRACT INGREDIENTS, WHAT IS EXPRESS AND IMPLIED TERMS

the new oxford companion to law, peter cane & Joanne conaghan, pub. oxford university press. isbn 978-0-19-929054-3

CONTRACT LAW means part of the CIVIL LAW that governs the enforceability of agreements. LEGAL OBLIGATION which arise from CONTRACTS are SELF IMPOSED and RELATE to INDIVIDUALS' CONDUCT in CRIMINAL LAW and LAW OF TORT. INDIVIDUAL (S) or ORGANISATION who ENTER into a CONTRACT have OBLIGATIONS TO ACT FOR ANOTHER'S BENEFIT e.g. paying money, rendering services or delivering goods. IN CONTRACT LAW THE LAW HAS TO IDENTIFY 1)When OBLIGATIONS arise, the 2) CONTENTS of such OBLIGATIONS and the 3) LEGAL CONSEQUENCES OF THEIR BREACH.

AGREEMENT IN WRITING IS NEEDED FOR A CONTRACT TO EXIST BUT ALSO ORAL EXCHANGES (VERBAL CONTRACT e.g. a promise by promisor K to pay promisee Q for legal advise on erecting a fence that the neighbour U wants to take K to court over), CONTRACT CAN BE MERE CONDUCT, A CONTRACT CAN BE DURABLE FORMS e.g. WRITING OR ELECTRONIC STORAGE. A WRITTEN CONTRACT IS NECESSARY FOR LAND. CONSIDERATION IS NECESSARY IN A CONTRACT unless the PROMISE is contained in a DEED. CONSIDERATION is something has to be given in return for a promise to be legally enforceable. THE COURT OF WILL NOT EXCEPT OR ENFORCE *GRATUITOUS PROMISE e.g. a promise of a gift is made without CONSIDERATION.

A BINDING CONTRACT means an AGREEMENT is needed before TRANSFER OF GOODS AND SERVICES TAKES PLACE.

A CONTRACT that is not PERFORMED AS AGREED, one party may request a court to enforce the AGREEMENT.

LAND CONTRACT means a court may compel a transfer of the LAND to the purchaser by an order of SPECIFIC PERFORMANCE of the CONTRACT. A BREACH OF CONTRACT THE REMEDY WILL CONSIST OF PAYMENT but not for CONTRACTS THAT CONCERN LAND. COMMON CLAIM FOR BREACH IS FOR PRICE DUE UNDER CONTRACT, monetary COMPENSATION is DAMAGES. DAMAGES can be claimed when goods or services are not provided as agreed in the contract.

DAMAGES means loss suffered by CLAIMANT which measured by comparing the CLAIMANT'S position if the CONTRACT had been properly performed.

CLAIMANT is expected to take reasonable steps to 'MITIGATE' LOSSES, and is limited to COMPENSATION for losses which could have been FORESEEN.

A PARTY may RESCIND (END) a CONTRACT was procured by WRONGDOING e.g. MISREPRESENTATION OF CONTRACT OR DURESS e.g. UNDUE INFLUENCE THAT IS 1) EXPRESSED INFLUENCE means that the party seeking to avoid the transaction must prove IMPROPER PRESSURE by the advantaged person induced to make a CONTRACT, and 2) UNDUE INFLUENCE OF ADVANTAGE PERSON being the type of SPECIAL RELATIONSHIP where one party is better educated, dominant PSYCHOLOGICAL INFLUENCE or has a SENIOR RELATIONSHIP to the other party. see O'Sullivan v Management Agency & Music International [1985] QB 428. cited in p122 pub. old bailey press Obligations: Contract Law , vickneswaren krishnan , ISBN 1858364671.

MISTAKE of a CONTRACT remedies BREACH OF A CONTRACT of which can be applied because there was no CONTRACT at all.
At common law the effect of an operative MISTAKE is to render the CONTRACT VOID an initio, no matter how BLAMELESS the parties are or how the MISTAKE arose. NO OBLIGATIONS can arise under such a contract, nor can title in goods (p103 obligations: contract law, ISBN 1858364671, vickneswaren krishnan, pub. old bailey press).
There three main groups of MISTAKE at common law: 1) COMMON MISTAKE to -
i. the existence of the subject matter of the contract (red extincta), see MacRae v Commonwealth Disposals Common (1951) 84 CLR 377; ii. the belief as to ownership (red sua) see Cooper v Phibbs (1987) LR 2 2HL 149; and iii. belief as to the qualit see Bell v lever Bros (1932) AC 161. 2) MUTUAL MISTAKE can be defined as occurring where the two parties have reached genuine agreement, but under some common misapprehension as to the FACT which lies at the heart of the contract, see Bell v Lever Bros Ltd. 3) UNILATERAL MISTAKE occurs where although apparently the parties have AGREED, in fact there is no genuine AGREEMENT between them, hence NO BINDING CONTRACT.

Example - A wrote to B OFFERING to sell his car for £5,000. B assumed A was referring to A's Austin car worth £6,000 whereas, in fact, A was referring to the Morris worth £4,500.

TRITE LAW means an OFFER can be revoked at any time before ACCEPTANCE. PUFF means an expression or opinion. A mere PUFF is not construed as a REPRESENTATION see Dimmock v Gallery (1866) 2 CH App 21, simple expression of opinion is not taken as REPRESENTATION OF CONTRACT , see Bisset v Wilkinson (1927) AC 177. EXAMPLE - R, a car dealer, agreed to sell a car to S for £5,000 after S had examined the car on the garage forecourt. The document on the car windscreen indicated the price and in large letters said ' ALL OUR CARS ARE IN TIP TOP CONDITION (A PUFF)'. In small print was a clause which read, 'we accept no legal responsibility for the condition of the vehicle. For TERMS of SALE see notice in the office and the details in the SALE AGREEMENT' (EXCLUSION OR EXEMPTION CLAUSES are attempts by ONE PARTY OR OTHER to EXCLUDE (wholly or partially) liability for the happening of certain events e.g. trade PUFF).

peter darwent, Ian yule, aqa2 law unit3, criminal law - offences against the person and contract law, pub. Philip Allan, ISBN 978-1-4441-7373-4 , www.philipallan.co.uk/studentunitguides

p61 FORMATION OF A CONTRACT:

*ISSUES OF OFFER AND ACCEPTANCE - what constitute an OFFER (OFFER - the expression or willingness to enter into a legally binding agreement see Carlill v Carbolic Smoke Ball Company (1996) where an ADVERTISEMENT may constitute an OFFER to the world i.e. to anyone who reads it JUDGE Bowen LJ gave the OBITER DICTA OR OBITER DICTUM THAT a lost dog reward is OFFER to whole world, OFFER is a CONTRACT. More recent common law precedent case see Bowerman v ABTA (1996)) - ACCEPTANCE see Felthouse v Bindley (1862) rules on ACCEPTANCE, ACCEPTANCE must be communicated, mere silence cannot be accepted, COURTS WILL INTERPRET ACCEPTANCE can be inferred from ***CONDUCT (BEHAVIOUR)*** see Brogden v Metropolitan Rail Co. (1877) , METHODS OF ACCEPTANCE (POSTAL RULE , ACCEPTANCE is valid when letter is posted even if the letter is lost in the post , but a REVOCATION of an OFFER is VALID ONLY WHEN THE LETTER IS RECEIVED see Adams v Lindsell (1818), INSTANTANEOUS METHODS OF ACCEPTANCE e.g. telephone, fax, or telex see Entores v Miles Far East Corporation (1955) and Brinkibon v Stahag Stahl (1983), (unqualified and unconditional acceptance of all the terms of the offer) - INVITATION TO TREAT ( ) - unilateral contracts ( ) - postal rule and modern methods of communication ( ) - reform ( )

*CONSIDERATION / CONSIDERATION ISSUES see Currie v miss (1875) - market value (must have some value) - must not be past - existing duty (must not be existing duty) - part payment of debts ( ) - PROMISSORY ESTOPPEL ( ) - reform ( )

- PROMISSORY ESTOPPEL - the principle that if a promisor makes a promise, which another person acts on, the promisor is stopped from breaking the promise, even if the other party did not provide CONSIDERATION.

- REFORM - although CONSIDERATION is required as it allows parties to escape liability. In 1937 Law Revision Committee proposed reforms to CONSIDERATION that - a written promise should always be binding, with or without CONSIDERATION - that past CONSIDERATION should be valid - that performance of an existing duty should be good CONSIDERATION - a CREDITOR should be bound by a PROMISE to accept part-payment in full settlement of a debt. To date none of these proposals has been adopted.

*INTENTION TO CREATE LEGAL RELATIONS - presumed in COMMERCIAL and BUSINESS agreements (parties involved intend agreement to be legally bound see Esso Petroleum v Customs and Excise Commissioners (1976) , McGowan v Radio Buxton (2001)) but not in SOCIAL OR DOMESTIC ARRANGEMENTS (agreements within families see Jones v Padavatton, contrast Balfour v Balfour (1919) and Merritt v Merritt (1970), social arrangement see Simpkins v Pays (1955), Peck v Late (1973) and Parker v Clarke (1960)).

/

p50
CONTRACT TERMS - these are statements incorporated in a contract.

CONDITIONS - CONDITIONS ARE TERMS THAT ARE FUNDAMENTAL TO A CONTRACT. A BREACH of a CONDITION will give the injured party the choice of either REPUDIATING (ENDING) the CONTRACT or CONTINUING with it and CLAIMING DAMAGES. CONDITIONS go to the root of the contract and result in REPUDIATION (right to REJECT goods and demand the return of the purchase price. This right to reject is lost when the goods have been accepted, and claim then is limited to damages; see s.11(4) of the 1979 Act) of the contract.

WARRANTIES - WARRANTIES ARE LESS IMPORTANT TERMS AND, IF BROKEN, ENTITLE AN INJURED PARTY ONLY TO DAMAGES - WARRANTIES are less and important terms and give rise only to DAMAGES.

DAMAGES - may be more appropriate than REJECTION when supplies of the product are limited and buying an alternative is difficult, or where call consumers have suffered personal injury because of faulty product and wish to sue for consequential LOSS (for LOSS awarded sums far exceeding the value of the product see Grant v Australian Knitting Mills (1936) and Godley v Perry (1960)).

INNOMINATE TERMS - are more flexible and can be treated as CONDITIONS (serious breach see Poussard v Spiders and Pond (1876), or WARRANTIES (minor breach see Bettini v Gye (1876)).

EXPRESS TERMS - are those things specifically agreed.

IMPLIED TERMS - are those added by the law. The most important important IMPLIED TERMS are those ADDED BY STATUTE (ACTS OF PARLIAMENT LEGISLATION) under the SALE OF GOODS ACT 1979 and the SUPPLY OF

GOODS AND SERVICES ACT 1982. specific STATUTORY remedies are available for breaches of these terms.

EXEMPTION CLAUSES - seek to exclude or limit LIABILITY. COMMON LAW controls (see L'Estrange v Graucob (1934) rule applies if other party has not MISREPRESENTED the terms of the agreement. see MISREPRESENTATION in Curtis v Chemical Cleaning and Dyeing Co. (1951))require the clause to be incorporated in the CONTRACT and drawn to the attention of the other party. UNFAIR CONTRACT TERMS ACT 1977 and UNFAIR TERMS IN CONSUMER CONTRACTS REGULATIONS 1999 regulate exemption clauses in consumer contracts.

*CONTRACT TERMS - issues with conditions, warranties and innominate terms ( ) - issues with statutory implied terms ( ) - issues with exemption clauses ( )

REMEDIES - damages (   ) - equitable remedies ( ) - remedies for breach of implied terms

/

**MISREPRESENTATION - is a VITIATING FACTOR (means has the effect making consent invalid or not valid or not true). A CONTRACT may be declared VOID on the grounds of MISREPRESENTATION (untrue statement of fact that induces a party to enter a contract but is not itself part of the contract see Walters v Morgan (1861) , Peek v Gurney (1873), half-true statement , misleading impression by being incomplete see Dimmock v Hallett (1866) and Spice Girls Ltd v Aprilia (2000). MISREPRESENTATION - can be FRAUDULENT MISREPRESENTATION (when a party makes a false statement without honestly believing it to be true, see Derry v Peek (1889)) , - can be NEGLIGENT MISREPRESENTATION (when principle of LIABILITY (failure to act) is based on the DUTY OF CARE in TORT arising proof of special relationship exist between the parties e.g carer, doctor, police officer. see rule / rule of law in common law case precedent created b Judges Hedley Byrne v Heller (1964) , in Statute Acts of Parliament Legislation created by parliament dratfsmen Section 2(1) MISREPRESENTATION ACT 1967) , can be INNOCENT MISREPRESENTATION - made innocently with honest belief in its truth e.g. repeating inaccurate information supplied by someone else - action brought in EQUITY (fairness) for RECESSION (equitable remedy that may be exercised by the innocent party by informing the other party of his intention to RESCIND / END the contract or by applying to the court for an order of RECISSION. The effect of this REMEDY RECISSION EQUITABLE REMEDY IS TO PUT THE PARTIES BACK INTO THE POSITION THEY WERE IN BEFORE THE CONTRACT WAS MADE. COMMON LAW REMEDY OF DAMAGES IS AVAILABLE. THE EQUITABLE REMEDY ARE AVAILABLE AT THE COURT'S DISCRETION. p392 ISBN 0333727800, Brenda mother sole and Ann ridley , a level law in action, pub. Macmillan, WWW.macpress.com).

//..//

TORT (OLD FRENCH) means CIVIL WRONG , WRONG OR INJURY.

TORT emanating Medival Latin, TORTUM means INJUSTICE (etymoogical root of TORTURE).

Tort Law - Principal mechanism for the provision of COMPENSATION for PERSONAL INJURIES - through the TORT of NEGLIGENCE.

TORTS take the form of scurrilous attacks on a person's reputation (DEFAMATION); Deliberate physical harm (TRESPASS to PERSON); or calling a STRIKE (inducing BREACH OF CONTRACT).

THE EMERGENCE OF NEW TORTS RECOGNISED SOCIAL PROBLEM SUCH AS HARASSMENT.

A CIVIL WRONG is a breach of a CIVIL OBLIGATION by ONE PARTY entitling another PARTY TO SUE.

CIVIL OBLIGATION and its BREACH is a matter of COMMON LAW drawn from centuries of DECISION-MAKING, although TORT has been subject of LEGISLATION e.g. in STATUTE ' occupiers' duties to visitors and trespassers (Occupiers' Liability Act 1954 and 1984) and DISCRIMINATION CLAIMS.

TORT seeks to protect three types of interest:

(1) interest to PROPERTY - primary TORTS are PRIVATE NUISANCE (The UNREASONABLE interference with the use and enjoyment of PROPERTY RIGHTS);

TRESPASSER - Entering a building WITHOUT PERMISSION

Trespass to LAND or GOODS;

Negligence causing PROPERTY DAMAGE e.g. To your car.

(2) interests in PERSONAL SECURITY AND INTEGRITY - NEGLIGENCE causing PERSONAL INJURY, the TORTS (WRONG) comprising TRESPASS to a person (ASSAULT, BATTERY, and FALSE IMPRISONMENT), and the TORTS governing DAMAGE to REPUTATION (SLANDER and LIBEL, comprising the law of DEFAMATION); and

(3) ECONOMIC INTERESTS - in profit, capital investment, and economic expectation. PROTECTION OF ECONOMIC INTERESTS mostly around INDUSTRIAL ACTION to PROSCRIBE AND DELIMIT THE SCOPE OF LEGITIMATE CONDUCT. also HARMFUL BUSINESS PRACTICES eg earliest ECONOMIC TORTS IS INDUCING BREACH OF CONTRACT see Lumley v Wagner (1852) where a theatre director's efforts to 'POACH' a singer from a business competitor.

ECONOMIC HARM - TORT OF DECEIT is a false statement of existing FACT made with knowledge of its FALSITY and the intention that it should be acted upon to the DETRIMENT OF THE CLAIMANT.

ECONOMIC TORTS understood as basic rules governing BUSINESS TRANSACTIONS, rules containing the COLLECTIVE INDUSTRIAL STRENGTH OF WORKERS ENGAGED IN STRIKES.

TORT LAW is about INDIVIDUAL AND SOCIAL RESPONSIBILITY.

REMEDY INDIVIDUAL WRONG IS THE FORM A CLAIM WILL TAKE TO ADDRESS BROADER SOCIAL CONCERNS eg THE RIGHTS OF CONSUMERS, THE PROTECTON OF THE ENVIRONMENT AND/OR SOCIAL AND CULTURAL INEQUALITIES. Example - a claim in nuisance to limit the POLLUTING EMISSIONS OF A NEARBY FACTORY; one might seek to bring a CLAIM against the POLICE for poor investigation of RACIALLY MOTIVATED CRIME AS A WAY OF COMBATING THE PERCEIVED RACISM OF POLICE PRACTICES; one might SUE a SCHOOL for FAILING TO ADDRESS

EDUCATIONAL NEEDS OF A DYSLEXIC PEOPLE as part of a broader CAMPAIGN TO PROMOTE THE EDUCATIONAL RIGHTS OF THE DISABLED. HERE IN ALL THESE INSTANCES ALTHOUGH INDIVIDUAL RIGHTS HAVE BEEN VIOLATED, TORT LAW POSES AN OPPORTUNITY FOR WIDER POLITICAL ENGAGEMENT ABOUT SOCIAL ISSUES AND CONCERNS.

Some people disapprove of the idea of using TORT as a tool or instrument for bringing about social change.
Tort law is argued is about CORRECTING INJUSTICES arising from the breach of obligations owed to a particular party or parties; it is not concerned with ensuring a more JUST OR EQUITABLE DISTRIBUTION OF LOSSES AND GAINS IN WIDER SOCIETY.

/

ACTS which comprise a TORT may also be CRIMINAL (see above eg TRESPASS). IN NEGLIGENCE TORT LAW is better at protecting PHYSICAL INTERGRITY see above.
IN NEGLIGENCE TORT LAW struggles to recognise and remedy emotional HARM (psychological integrity).
It a question of recognising harm in SOCIAL, POLITICAL AND CULTURAL CONDITION.
changes in SOCIAL AND CULTURAL ATTITUDES - the courts have begun to view as potentially TORTIOUS HARMS which previously would have attracted no LIABILITY, eg DAMAGE TO EDUCATIONAL OPPORTUNITY see Phelps v Hillingdon LBC (2001) or interference with the integrity of family life (M v Newham BC (1995), a process of opening the parameters of REMEDIABLE HARM, which has been assisted by the IMPLEMENTATION of the HUMAN RIGHTS ACT and a heightened HUMAN RIGHTS CULTURE.

PRODUCT LIABILITY cases in TORT are subject to the ordinary rules of NEGLIGENCE see DONOGHUE v STEVENSON (1932), where CLAIMANT / PLAINTIFF Mrs Donoghue had to prove the DEFENDANT ginger beer manufacturer owed her a duty of care, that he had breached that DUTY and the BREACH was the cause of her gastroenteritis and nervous shock.
KEY to PRODUCT LIABILITY is proving that the DEFENDANT'S LACK OF REASONABLE CARE caused the DEFECT THAT MADE THE PRODUCT DANGEROUS, although the claimant does not need to prove exactly what the defendant did wrong, see Mason v Williams and Williams (1955).
THE CONSUMER PROTECTION ACT 1987 says if a CLAIMANT SUFFERS HARM AS A RESULT OF THE PRODUCT BEING DEFECTIVE, he or she may be ENTITLED TO SUE the manufacturer of that product for COMPENSATION without having to prove that the producer committed any kind of legal wrong in manufacturing that product.

Section 1(2) of the Consumer Product Act 1987says a PRODUCT - any goods or electricity or raw material see A v National Blood Authority (2001).
Under s.1(2), a PRODUCER is a manufacturer of the actual product or component, the importer of the product into EU, any person who brand names a product or by other means holds himself or herself out to be the producer.

DEFECT - means the defendant will be LIABLE FOR DAMAGE caused wholly or in part by a 'defect' in the product. COURT TAKES INTO ACCOUNT DEFECT eg MARKETED PRODUCT ; PACKAGING OF THE PRODUCT; USE OF ANY MARK - KITEMARK (reg) of BRITISH STANDARDS INSTITUTION IN RELATIOM TO THE PRODUCT; PRODUCT INSTRUCTIONS OR WARNING OR REFRAINING FROM DOING ANYTHING IN RELATION TO THE PRODUCT; WHAT MIGHT REASONABLY EXPECTED TO BE DONE WITH THE PRODUCT ; THE TIME WHEN THE PRODUCT WAS SUPPLIED BY ITS PRODUCER TO ANOTHER.

DEFENCES/ DEFENDANT - under s.4(1) of the Act - the DEFECT is attributable to compliance with a legal requiremen; The defendants did not any time supply the product to another. This proviso protects the defendants if the product has been stolen and then sold on to a customer who is injured because of a DEFECT; THE SUPPLY by the DEFENDANTS was not in the course of business nor was it SUPPLY with a view to profit; 'DEVELOPMENT RISKS' DEFENCE - the state of scientific and technical knowledge at the time when the PRODUCER put the product into circulation was not such as to enable the existence of the defect to be discovered.

//...//

EQUITY AS A SYSTEM OF LAW - Equity is centred on COMMON LAW legal system. EQUITY is a body of law. EQUITY evokes ideas of FAIRNESS and JUSTICE.
The HISTORY OF EQUITY'S DEVELOPMENT - In MEDIEVAL TIMES, ENGLISH 'COMMON LAW' was administered in royal courts established by the king. because
The law in these courts was 'COMMON LAW' because, in theory, IT APPLIED UNIVERSALLY. Individuals dissatisfied with the outcome in these courts could PETITION the King , alleging that the RULES had worked an INJUSTICE in their case. Since the King was regarded as the fount of JUSTICE, these pleas needed a considered response. The task was delegated to the Chancellor, the King's most powerful minister and Equity grew out of this delegated function. He could order individuals not to act upon their COMMON LAW RIGHTS but, instead, to act in some other more fair or just way. The precise form was at the Chancellor's discretion. The King's early reliance on the Chancellor had an important impact EQUITY'S DEVELOPMENT. In medieval times the Chancellor was usually AN CLERIC, familiar with ECCLESIASTICAL LAW and notions of NATURAL JUSTICE, and instinctively concerned about matters of conscience, conscience is a hallmark of EQUITY.

EQUITY WAS ONLY CALLED UPON TO INTERVENE WHEN THE COMMON LAW RULES WERE SEEN AS INADEQUATE.
Equity might declare a contract not binding even though it was binding a common law, or declare that a PARTY OWED OBLIGATION OF CONFIDENTIALITY NOT RECOGNISED IN COMMON LAW. When it came to REMEDIES, equity largely ignored the COMMON LAW PRACTICE OF MONEY REMEDIES, and typically ordered the defendant to do something, to hand over an item of property, perform a CONTRACT, cease creating a nuisance, or sign a document. If enforcement of these orders was needed, equity did not follow the common law

practice of stripping wrongdoers of assets to the extent necessary to pay the damages owed, but instead regarded it as CONTEMPT OF COURT to refuse to comply with EQUITY'S ORDER. Historically, DEFENDANTS could be thrown into prison for such CONTEMPT, this was powerful persuasion to comply.

//...//

TRUST - is a legal mechanism by which English law recognises and enforces A SEPARATION BETWEEN THE LEGAL OWNERSHIP OF PROPERTY (TRUSTEE) AND THE BENEFICIARIES RIGHT TO ENJOY THE BENEFITS OF THAT PROPERTY.

The BENEFICIARIES have a right to exclude others from enjoying the benefit of that TRUST PROPERTY.

TRUST Is created by the TRUST's CREATOR (THE SETTLOR) ENTRUSTING PROPERTY to a TRUSTEE who EXPRESSLY (agreed) or IMPLIEDLY (created by STATUTE) undertakes to hold the TRUST PROPERTY for the benefit of the BENEFICIARIES in accordance with the terms of the TRUST INSTRUMENT, the TRUSTEE holds LEGAL TITLE to the PROPERTY but the BENEFICIAL ENTITLEMENT to the PROPERTY rests in the hands of the TRUST'S BENEFICIARIES.

EQUITY courts (that the BENEFICIARIES' ENTITLEMENT TO THE PROPERTY IS AN EQUITABLE INTEREST) and COMMON LAW courts HAVE JURISDICTION to enforce TRUSTS.

The undertaking may also be given by the SETTLOR without any TRANSFER OF PROPERTY TO A THIRD PARTY.

The person giving the undertaking become bound by the TERMS of the trust and becomes a TRUSTEE.

Once the TRUST has been CONSTITUTED, the SETTLOR no longer has any enforceable RIGHTS in respect of the TRUST PROPERTY unless the SETTLOR reserved such RIGHTS at the outset (eg by making himself or herself one of the BENEFICIARIES of the TRUST, or by including a RIGHT to revoke the TRUST as one of the TERMS of the TRUST).

TRUSTEE'S POWERS AND DUTIES are default RULES OF LAW which can be modified by AGREEMENT when the TERMS of the TRUST are SETTLED.

The AGREEMENT cannot be modified to remove the TRUSTEE'S irreducible CORE DUTY to PERFORM the TRUST honestly and in good faith for the benefit of the BENEFICIARIES - IF THE DUTY IS REMOVED THERE IS NO REAL TRUST.

Once the TRUST has been created, the TRUSTEE'S OBLIGATION to comply with the TERMS of the TRUST can be avoided only if all the BENEFICIARIES ARE OF MAJORITY AGE AND SOUND MIND, and are willing to consent to the TRUSTEE'S CONDUCT, or if the court provides its consent to the conduct. The consent is variation of the TERMS OF TRUST.

The TRUSTEE is capable of being one of the BENEFICIARIES, should the SETTLOR so wish; but the TRUSTEE cannot be sole beneficiary under EQUITY.

The TRUST PROPERTY does not form part of the TRUSTEE'S beneficial patrimony hence TRUST is not available to pay his or her general CREDITORS in BANKRUPTCY.

//...//

EVIDENCE, CRIMINAL - In a criminal trial, the fact finder (who may be a LAY PERSON, such as a JUROR or MAGISTRATE, or a PROFESSIONAL JUDGE) must decide whether to find the DEFENDANT GUILTY.

A MISTAKEN GUILTY VERDICT will brand an INNOCENT PERSONAL A CRIMINAL, and may result in LOSS OF LIBERTY hence RULES are generally stricter than those governing civil trials.

STANDARD OF PROOF - means the FACT-FINDER should not return a VERDICT of GUILTY unless convinced BEYOND REASONABLE DOUBT of the DEFENDANT'S GUILT to protect DEFENDANTS from RISK of FALSE CONVICTION. Hence EVIDENCE may be EXCLUDED from a TRIAL even if it could promote ACCURATE DECISION MAKING eg IF THE EVIDENCE WAS OBTAINED IN BREACH OF THE SUSPECT'S RIGHTS. STANDARD OF PROOF required by criminal trials.

TWO TYPES of RULES OF EVIDENCE : 1) those promoting accurate decision-making ; 2) those concerned with FAIRNESS.

HEARSAY - the best known EXCLUSIONARY RULES EXCLUDE HEARSAY in the Anglo-American tradition. EVIDENCE is HEARSAY if it is EVIDENCE of a STATEMENT made BEFORE the TRIAL, and the person who made the STATEMENT is not available in court to be CROSS-EXAMINED about it.

Confrontation is a CONSTITUTIONAL RIGHT in the united States and receives some RECOGNITION in the EUROPEAN CONVENTION ON HUMAN RIGHTS, BRITISH courts have been reluctant to interpret it as a STRONG RIGHT because of RECOGNITION OF RIGHTS OF VICTIMS AND WITNESSES in the criminal process: courts are aware PROCESS OF GIVING EVIDENCE may be stressful, that in some cases witnesses face threats and intimidation.

The RULE against EVIDENCE of BAD CHARACTER protects DEFENDANTS from having their previous CONVICTIONS revealed in court (as HEARSAY RULE in England and Wales by Criminal Justice Act 2003).

Only relevant EVIDENCE is ADMISSIBLE. RELEVANT EVIDENCE is part of EMPIRICAL matter, eg a failure to respond to an accusation of wrongdoing is only relevant to the question of guilt if the guilty are more likely to stay silent than the innocent.

TYPES OF EVIDENCE - ADMISSIBLE EVIDENCE MAKE TAKE ONE OF SEVERAL FORMS : 1) TESTIMONY - oral evidence of a witness (direct testimony), or what another person perceived and witness is reporting that to the court as EVIDENCE OF TRUTH (a HEARSAY accepted or admissible under Civil Evidence Act 1968); 2) DOCUMENTARY EVIDENCE eg document in writing but also photographs, maps, plans drawings, blue-prints, cassettes, micro-dots etc. The document may be admitted because its content or existence is relevant; 3) REAL EVIDENCE comprises objects produced for inspection by the court in order that the court may draw inferences - evidence from the condition, existence etc of the object rather of its contents; 4) CIRCUMSTANTIAL EVIDENCE (facts from which an INFERENCE may or may not be drawn as to the FACT IN ISSUE) may be contrasted with 'DIRECT' EVIDENCE (some fact in issue of which the WITNESS has 'DIRECT' or FIRST-HAND KNOWLEDGE)

//...//

EUROPEAN UNION (EU) LAW

KEY POINTS - THE TREATIES FOUNDING THE EUROPEAN COMMUNITY :
1) The European Coal and Steel Community (ECSC) Treaty was to establish a common market for coal and steel products. ECSC TREATY was signed in Paris on 18 April 1951 and consists of 100 Articles, three annexes and three protocols; 2) The European Economic community (EC) Treaty was signed in Rome on 25 March 1957 and consists of 248 Articles, four annexes, three protocols. Article 2 identified four objects - promotion of harmonious economic development throughout the community - continuous and balanced economic expansion among the Member States - the raising of standards of living among the population of the Community - the development of closer relations among the Member States; 3)The European Atomic Energy (Euratom) Treaty signed in Rome on 25 March 1957 and contains 225 Articles. Main goals - to promote research and to ensure the dissemination of technical information throughout the Community - to establish uniform safety standards to protect workers and general public from atomic hazards - to promote investment in the nuclear energy industry - to maintain regular and reliable supplies of ores and nuclear fuels - to make certain that nuclear materials are not diverted for aims other than PEACEFUL PURPOSES.

STRUCTURE OF THE EUROPEAN COMMUNITY - The EC Treaty seeks to achieve the creation of the common market by pursuing four fundamental principles - free movement of the factors of production eg goods, labour, services and capital within the territory of the community - progressive approximation of economic policies among member States - the creation of a Common Customs Tariff (CCT) for the regulation and administration of trade between Community and non-Community countries - establishment of a Common Commercial Policy (CCP) for the conduct of economic relations between the Community and the rest of the world.
THE SINGLE EUROPEAN ACT - is an international agreement among the Member States of the Community and not a STATUTE of the British Parliament - reaffirmed the political objectives of the Community.

Where there is THE NATURE OF EUROPEAN COMMUNITY LAW (EU LAW) overrides BRITISH PARLIAMENTARY LAW and prevails over the of all Member States including England.

THE TREATY ON EUROPEAN UNION 1992 AND THE FUTURE EVOLUTION OF THE COMMUNITY - The European Community is presently undergoing a process of transformation from a primarily economic organisation into a true European Union. This transformation is to be brought about the Treaty on European Union signed in February 1992 at Maastricht.

THE AMENDED EC TREATY AND THE COMPETENCIES ESTABLISHED IN RELATION TO POLITICAL, ECONOMIC, MONETARY AND FISCAL AFFAIRS.
THE INTER-GOVERNMENTAL CONFERENCE AND REVISION TO THE TEU AND EC TREATY, see Costa v ENEL (1964) ECR 585 - The Community Treaties have established a new legal order stemming from the limitation of sovereignty or a transfer of powers from the Member States to the European Community and have thus created a body of law which binds both their nationals and themselves.

//...//

CHAPTER 2 - RAYCHELLIE took economics4makeup class to learn more about market structure of monopoly market and perfect competition competitive market tutorials IN ADDITION - fdd202 - TMA01 Demand Curve, Minimum Efficient Scale M.E.S. sa3aug16 - fdd202 - TMA02 game theory,monopoly,competition saaug16 - fdd202 - TMA03 labor Supply&Demand, income distribution-tues27may08 - fdd202 - TMA04 AD, stock market wealth, accelerator model - fdd202 - TMA05 int'l trade, int'l finance - fdd202 – TMA06 – MACROECONOMIC Inflation, Economic Growth, fdd202 - TMA06 inflat, interest rate, investment unemployment.

LORENZ CURVE, GINI COEFFICIENT, MEAN, STANDARD DEVIATION.

//

Read all the notes following the questions before planning any of your answers.

1a Draw the market demand curve corresponding to the data in Table 1, and show in your diagram what would happen to the quantity of wine demanded if the price rose from £4 to £9 a bottle.

<u>**Please refer to Separate sheet attached (Diagram 1)**</u>

If the price of the bottle of wine rose from £4 to £9, the Law of Demand (noted by Dawson et al p50) suggests that Ceritis Paribus - all things (such as income, tastes, expectations) being equal except for price, as price of the bottle of wine rises from £4 to £9, the demand for the bottle of wine will fall. This is represented by a movement along the demand curve.

Similarly: $P1 \times Q1 \rightarrow £4 \times 260 = £1040$ and $P2 \times Q2 \rightarrow £9 \times 260 = £1890$ (as shown in Diagram 1)

Following, the Demand for the Good (bottle of wine) at £9 is '**Price Inelastic**' because the demand for the bottle of wine at £4 is greater than the demand for wine the bottle of wine at £9. Thus the '**Marginal Revenue**' is '**Negative**' for the bottle of wine at £9.00 because no profit is made that exceeds those when the bottle of wine was at £4.

bb

1b Use the data in Table 2 to draw another diagram showing how the demand for wine is related to income. Assuming price is unchanged at £9, what would happen to the market demand for wine if average income were to rise? Explain, using a diagram, how this rise in income would affect the demand curve.

Please refer to Separate sheet attached (Diagram 2, using Data in Table 2)

Please refer to Separate sheet attached (Diagram 3)

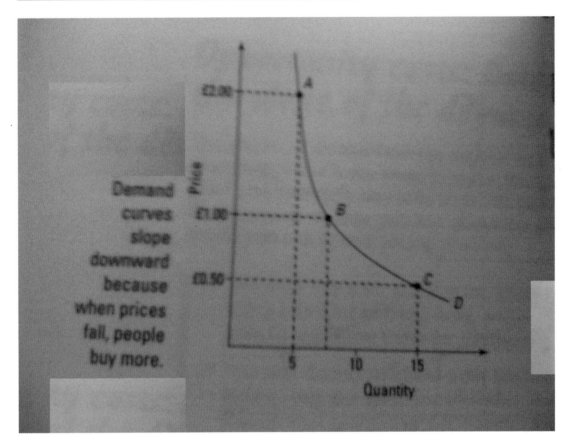

Assuming the price of the bottled of wine is unchanged and average income were to rise, the market demand for the normal good (noted by Dawson et al p51) or a luxury good such as the bottle of wine will increase. Hence, the rise in income will change the demand curve (as shown in Diagram 3) causing the demand curve to shift Right reflecting an increase in demand for the bottle of wine at a higher price £9.

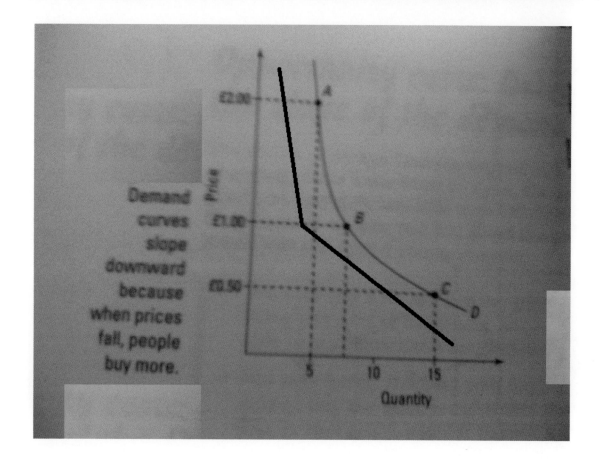

This is because according to Veblen's theory (The *Theory of the Leisure Class*, Veblen, 1912, in Dawson et al, p50), **'Conspicous Consumption'** will make consumers want to noticeably display their wealth to gain recognition from others as their status increases with income and will buy expensive goods such as the bottle of wine at £9 to reflect this status.

1c Using the data in Tables 3 and 4, draw (i) a diagram showing the market demand for tickets, and (ii) another diagram showing the relationship between income and the number of tickets purchased.

Please refer to Separate sheets attached (Diagram 4 and Diagram 5)

39

1d Do these data indicate that coach travel between London and the northern city is an inferior good? Explain your answer. (30%)

These data in Tables 3 and 4 and Digrams 4 and 5 indicate that Coach travel between London and the Northern City is an **'Inferior Good'**. This is because Table 3 and Diagram 4 shows that as Price of Coach travel to these two cities rises, demand falls and even when Income increases as shown in Table 4 and Diagram 5 and price of the Coach tickets remains at £2 – very cheap, demand still falls.

Likewise, one can apply the theory of the **'economic man'** that when income rises, consumers can afford to travel by more luxury means (i.e. Train travel) rather than cheaper inferior means (Coach travel). Thus the theory of the **'economic man'** suggests that consumers will maximise their utility/satisfaction according to their budget constraints and when consumers' income rise, consumers will choose to travel by quicker alternative means (i.e. Train travel) rather than by Coach which often has long congestion on the motorway.

2a Draw a market demand curve for turkey meat and show, on your diagram, the effect of the outbreak of bird flu reported in Extract 1 below.

Please refer to Separate sheet attached (Diagram 6)

2b Explain, using appropriate diagrams, how the bird flu scare affected demand for (i) chicken, and (ii) other meat. (30%)

2b (i) Please refer to Separate sheet attached (Diagram 7)

The Bird flu scare causes the Demand Curve for Chicken Meat to shift left to suggests that consumers (according to Extract 1) are convinced that bird meat like Chicken is unsafe, thus demand decreases at D_1 for Chicken Meat as shown on Diagram 7.

2b (ii) Please refer to Separate sheet attached (Diagram 8)

The Bird flu scare causes the Demand Curve for other meat to shift Right to suggest that consumers (according to extract 1) are convinced that bird meat like Turkey and Chicken are unsafe. Thus consumers look to other alternative meat (i.e. red meat) hence the Demand for other meat (particularly beef, a red meat which is considered a luxury for a Sunday roast dinner) increases at D_1 on Diagram 8.

3a Explain what is meant by 'long-run average cost' and draw a diagram to show how the long-run average cost curve's shape reflects returns to scale.

Please refer to Separate sheet attached (Diagram 9)

Long-run average cost is the long-running cost of a firm after its first stage/ birth stage in the industry. Long-run average costs assume that all a firm's factors (such as cutting costs, increasing wages in line with Government policy increases on Mininum wage etc) are variables and thus are likely to change.

For instance, Diagram 9 shows how Long-run average cost curve reflects returns to scale. For example, if a firm were to employ techonology that would increase bulk supplies (output) i.e. fridges, washing machines to provide cheaper costs to consumers, the firms Long-run average costs would be operating at an **Increasing Returns to Scale (Economies of Scale)** because as output increases, the costs reduces.

Also, after a period of time, if the firm is not able to cut any further costs, then the firm's **costs remain unchanged/constant (Constant Returns to Scale).**

Nonetheless, if consumers are tired of having the same items in bulk and want more fashionable individualised products / goods (like Large American Fridges with Juice dispensers) to suit their lifestyle and increase in income, then the firm will no longer be able to shift the bulk supplies / goods then the firm is no longer productive as not enough money is made to cater for i.e. maintenance and repairs of machinery/techonology and wages so the firms costs begin to rise causing a firms costs to operate at a Decreasing Returns to Scale (diseconomies of scale) since output is high and costs are also high.

3b How can the existence of a minimum efficient scale of production affect the number and size of firms in an industry? Read Extract 2 and Extract 3 and illustrate your answer with reference to the motor and ready-made food industries.

The existence of Minimum Efficient Scale (M.E.S where a firm reaches its minimum level of costs as output rises), can affect the number of firms and size of firms in an industry. For example, with the existence of M.E.S, a lot of smaller firms like Noon Curry King ready-made food as shown in Extract 3 will be at an advantage because they they will be able to operate a niche market (and meet the individual needs of consumers lifestyle). This is because, with the existence of M.E.S, there will be no scope for the fewer big businesses / firms (with merges with other firms, 'super-league' as Extract 2 calls it) like Ford motors (which includes Mazda, Jaguar and Volvo) to operate because there comes a point where bigger businesses /firms cannot drive down any more costs as output increases becase they are too large.

3c How would your analysis in (b) above be modified if (i) there were no minimum efficient scale, and (ii) if the demand for a product were affected by network externalities? (40%)

3c(i) No Minimum Effcient Scale (M.E.S) would mean that 'super-league' big firms would be able to operate in the market, because 'super-league' firms like Ford will be able to update their technology every time to meet consumer demands for Individualised fashionable goods. This in turn would price smaller firms out of the market because the bigger firms would be able to produce the Individualised fashionable goods that the smaller firms are producing but at a cheaper and more competitive price.

3c(ii) Network Externalities is where more people join the same service to get i.e. cheaper deals with other service users. If the demand for a producet were affected Network Externalties, the fewer big firms like Ford motors would be at an advantage as they have vertically integrated to control all stages of management, production and distribution so if a consumer's Ford car breaks down, Ford with a number of garages all over England, the consumer will get a cheaper and competitive price on the repair of their Ford car if they took their broken down car to a Ford Garage than to a smaller private/independent Garage.

Word Count

1,094 words

References

- Collin, P.H. (2005, reprint), 'Bloomsbury Reference Dictionary of Law', London, Bloomsbury Publishing Plc,

- Dawson, G., Mackintosh, M., Anand, P. (2006),, Economics and Economic Change: Microeconomics, Milton Keynes, The Open Univerity.

- DD202 Tutor-marked Assignments 2008 Booklet (2007) The Open University

- Veblen, T. (1912) The Theory of the Leisure Class, Macmillan, London **in** Dawson, G., Mackintosh, M., Anand, P. (2006),, Economics and Economic Change: Microeconomics, Milton Keynes, The Open Univerity.

- Callaghan, G., Fribbance, I., Higginson, M (2007), 'Personal Finance', Milton Keynes, The Open University

Conspicuous consumption (noticeable consumption) : The ostentatious (flamboyant) display of wealth in order to gain recognition by others of an increase in one's status. p92

Thorstein Veblen, an American institutional economist, analysed cultural influences on consumption. In *The Theory of the Leisure Class* (Veblen, 1912) he suggested that it can be important to show off your wealth by means of conspicuous consumption.

Calculating is a borrowed paradigm/model or feature of the *'economic man'* in Economics who simply seeks to maximise his or her utility and therefore will calculate his purchases in light of his/her tastes for products and the relative prices of those products from. Collins Dictionary of Economics

dd202 - TMA01 Demand Curve, Min Efficient Scale – tues11mar08

//

1a Does Extract 1 below suggest that Scottish dairy farming more closely resembles a monopoly or a perfectly competitive industry? Give at least two reasons for your answer.

From extract 1, the first paragraph indicates that the Extract is about 'Scottish Dairy Farmers' and goes further in the third paragraph to say that *"there are...1,400 dairy farmers left"* in the Scottish dairy farming industry.

These Extracted passages above suggest that Scottish dairy farming resembles a <u>perfectly competitive industry</u> because firstly there are many sellers (1,400 dairy farmers) as well as buyers/consumers since milk is mass-consumed. Secondly, the good (milk) offered by the various Scottish dairy farmers are largely the same (homogenous) as the product sold by the various dairy farmers and cannot be distinguished from one another. For example, pints of milk sold by one dairy farmer looks like a pint of milk sold by another dairy farmer.

The Extract goes further to say that the *"In 2004 the average UK milk price received by the farmer was 18.5p* [per litre, and]...*farmers should join together into co-operatives to process milk if they want a greater share of profit"*. Thus, thirdly, this suggests that the Scottish dairy farming resembles a perfectly competitive industry because the Scottish dairy farmers are price-takers (cannot influence price due to their position in the market, making-up a very small proportion of the total market) and so they take the price determined by the industry/market for milk.

Fourthly, the Extract states that *"[t]here are 1,400 dairy farmers left in Scotland....There were almost 5,000 producers about 20 years ago"*. This suggests that Scottish dairy farming resembles a perfectly competitive industry as the 3,600 out of 5,000 farmers who have been free to 'exit' the Scottish dairy farming industry.

1b Use an appropriate diagram to explain why even loss-making farmers may remain in the industry in the short run.

Please refer to separate sheet attached.

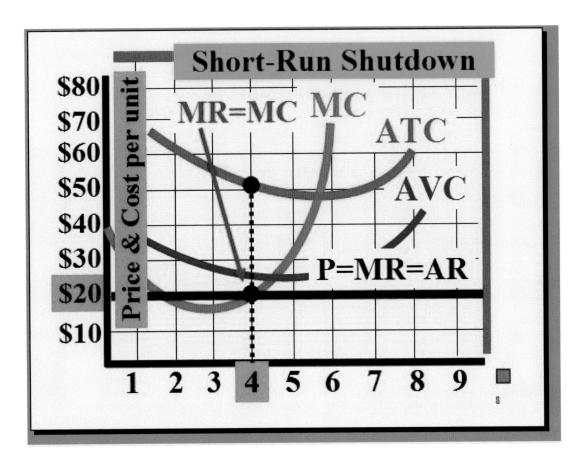

The graph shows that the competitive firm/farmer would follow their goal of **'maximising profits'** by producing quantity at which Marginal Cost (MC) equals Marginal Revenue (MR) → MC = MR, where MR is the change in total revenue from an additional one unit sold; and Marginal Cost is the Competitive Firm/Farmer's (short-run) Supply Curve.

Similarly the graph shows Average Revenue, AR as being equal to MR (and MC). Average Revenue is the total revenue divided by the quantity sold and hence this calculation indicates how much revenue a farmer recieves fro one unit sold.

The graph also shows that, when Average Variable Cost (AVC) or Short-run Average Variable Cost (SRAVC)is greater than Selling Price, P (P<AVC), this means that the revenue the firm/farmer gets from the price the milk is sold for is less than the (short-run) Average Variable Cost of production. Here the farmer has made a loss but can still remain in the industry providing the loss does not include Average Total Cost (ATC), whereby Average Total Cost is not more than Selling Price,P (P<ATC). If this was the case, the farmer/firm would have to exit the Scottish dairy farming industry/market because the farmer would be producing less revenue than its total cost – thus making an overall loss.

As the farmer is making a loss since P<AVC, the farmer may decide not to produce anything (i.e. **shut-down**) during a specific time period because of current market conditions whilst the market improves providing that Selling Price (P) equals Average Total Cost (ATC) or Short-run Average Total Cost (SRATC), as this means that exactly a normal profit (zero economic profit) is being made i.e. zero difference between Selling Price and Total Cost to produce.

1c Analyse the effect on the market price of a large number of farmers leaving the industry.

Please refer to separate sheet attached.

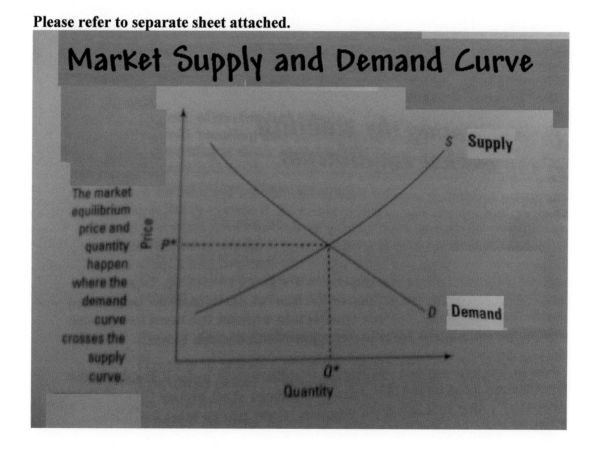

47

The Market Supply and Demand Curve shows that at S_1, there are many suppliers/farmers in the dairy farming industry (namely perfectly competititve market). Thus the quantity (supply) increases so that price reduces to P_1 to sell at quantity Q_1

However the Market Supply and Demand Curve also show that factors (other than price) such as a large number of farmers leaving the farming industry, causes the Supply Curve to shift left and upwards at S_2. At S_2, the supply for milk (quantity) reduces since there are less suppliers/farmers in the market and hence price increases at P_2.

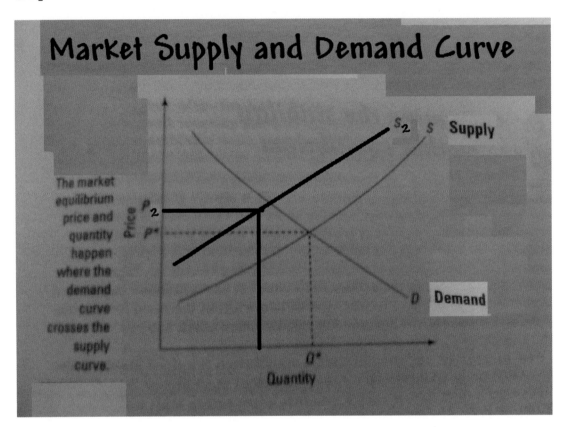

1d What level of long-run profits will be required by farmers to prevent them leaving the industry?

Please refer to separate sheet attached.

Graph shows that, when Selling Price (P) equals Average Total Cost (ATC) or Long-run Average Total Cost (LRATC), this means that exactly Long-run 'normal profits'(zero economic profit) is being made i.e. zero difference between Selling Price and Total Cost to produce. Hence, in zero economic profit equillibrium, the farmer is compensated by getting back in the form of the revenue he/she produces for the time and money in keeping his/her dairy farming firm going and so this would prevent farmers from leaving the industry. This is because if it was any other competitive market situation where i.e. Selling Price is greater than Average Total Cost (ATC) or Long-run Average Total Cost (LRATC): P>ATC, farmers would be making super-normal profits. Thus these farmers making super-normal profits would be making these super-normal profits in the short-run as these farmers making super-normal profits would be opening up opportunities for new entrants to: enter the Scottish Dairy industry/market; undercut existing prices (since price falls as supply increases because there are more farmers in the industry); and take the profits for themselves. This would encourage existing farmers to leave the Scottish Dairy farming Industry as they would be able to recover their original expenditure used to set up and run their farm with no **'sunk costs'** (sunk costs is irrecoverable costs incurred from setting up and running the business).

2a Calculate the combined profits of Tresco and Sudbury's for each of the four possible outcomes shown in Table 1 below.

Table 1
Pay-off matrix showing profits (£m) with and without loyalty cards

		Sudbury's:	
		no loyalty card	loyalty card
Tresco:	no loyalty card	100, 100	60, 120
	loyalty card	120, 60	80, 80

Table 1			
Pay-off matrix showing (£m) and combine profits (£m) with and without loyalty cards			
		Sudbury's:	
Tresco:		No loyalty card	Loyalty card
	no loyalty card	100,100 *(200)	60,120 *(180)
	loyalty card	120, 60 *(180)	80,80 *(160)
*combined profits of Tresco and Sudbury's			

2b Explain, using the concept of 'dominant strategy', which outcome is most likely.

Using the concept of 'dominant strategy', 'dominant strategy' (in game theory) is where one strategy gives a player a higher pay-off than any other strategy irrespecitve of what the other player does or if both players have a dominant strategy then the solution of the game is that each player plays their dominant strategy.

Thus using this strategy (dominant strategy), the outcome that is most likely is for Tresco and Sudbury's to both play their dominant strategy by not introducing loyalty cards. This is because Tresco and Sudbury's combined profits is highest at £200m – higher than any other pay-off on the matrix if both decide not to introduce loyalty cards.

2c Why are supermarkets faced with a dilemma when introducing loyalty cards? Who benefits from this dilemma?

Working out Tresco and Sudbury's comined loss:

$$200 - 160 = 40, \rightarrow \frac{40}{160} = 0.25, \rightarrow 0.25 \times 100\% = 25\%$$

As the matrix and above calculation shows, supermarkets are faced with a dilemma when introducing loyalty cards because as the matrix and above calculation shows, the two supermarkets Tresco and Sudbury's make a combined loss of 25% at £160m from £200m if they were to introduce loyalty cards than if they did not. Thus in this case, the consumer benefits from this dilemma because the two supermarkets are making a combined 25% less profits, 25% profits which goes to the consumer in the form of loyalty cards.

3 Explain how monopoly, in contrast to competition, can work to the detriment of the consumer. Contrast that view with the theory underlying the proposed changes in Irish competition policy outlined in Extract 2 below.

Monopoly, in constrast to competition, can work to the detriment of the consumer when a monopoly firm acts to maximise its profits like competitive firms.

For instance, Dawson et al look at the Microsoft (Windows Operating System) case and note *"abuse of monopoly power such as monopoly pricing and deliberate blocking of competition by 'predatory' behaviour against the interest of the consumers"*. (Dawson et al, 2006, p102).

Similarly, Also Gilbert and Katz, 2001 in Dawson et al, 2006 note that *"government emphasized the long-term potential damage to users from eliminating future competitive pressure on prices and quality"* (Dawson et al, 2006, p96).

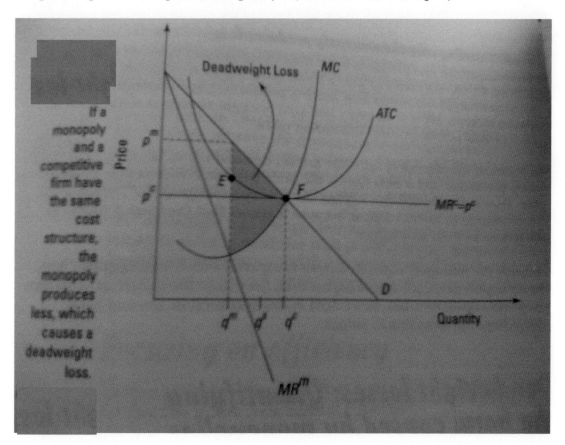

This means the monopoly firm sells its product (output) at a higher price (at Selling Price, P > MC, Marginal Cost) that it can get away with (price maker) unlike a competitive market which sells their product at the price (at Selling Price, P = MC, Marginal Cost which is the competitive firm's supply curve) determined by the market (price-taker). This monopoly can work to the detriment of the consumer because in contrast to the Competition policy outlined in Extract 2, in competitive market the act states that the *"essence of a competitive market is the ability for potential competitors to acutally compete which the market's leading firms"*, thus the consumer would be getting a competitive price. In monopoly, prices are higher for the consumer because the price is not a competitive one because it is set by the monopoly firm.

An example of consumer's not paying a competitive price (but instead a monopoly price) could be that as stated in Dawson et al whereby at one time, Netscape's Internet browser posed a potential competiton of Microsoft Internet Explorer browser. This is because Netscape along with Java language could *"grow into a layer of 'middleware' – software that lies between the operating system* [Windows Operating System] *and the software applications of interest to users from the underlying Operating System"*, thus removing the barrier to entry created by Microsoft as the sole producer as Netscape will gain Microsoft's users. However, Microsoft stopped this from occuring by pricing Netscape out ot the market via investing *"US $100 million per year during 1995-97 into iimproving its browser Internet Explorer"* (Dawson et al, 2006, p95) *"and paid Apple to use their browser"* (Klein, 2001 in Dawson et al, 2006, p95)

Also, the monopoly firm produces less quantity (output) than the perfectly competitive market. This can work to the detriment of the consumer because unlike in competitive market where more supply/quantity (output) lowers prices for the consumer in monopoly, prices are higher.

Additionally, the monopoly firms product (output) has a higher production cost and is not as efficiently produced as that of the perfectly compeitive market. In contrast the Competiton Policy outlined in Extract 2 states with compeition the *"benefits of increased competition are lower prices, greater choice for consumers (businesses as well as individuals) and enhanced innovation"*. Likewise, monopoly can work to the detriment of the consumer because the monopoly firm compromises on quality (enhanced innovation) and hence the consumer is not getting quality (enhanced innovation) for the high price they pay for the product. In other words, the consumer does not get value for money.

Alongside, the market failure of a monopoly power is caused by 'Deadweight loss' or 'Deadweight welfare loss', thus working to the detriment of the consumer. The Competition policy outlined in Extract 2 observes that *"there is welfare loss arising from monopoly power"*. This is because the monopoly produces output (quantity) below the accepted level produced by competiton / competitive market (as discussed above) and hence, Deadweight Loss is the loss of consumer surplus and producer surplus in a monopoly when compared with a perfectly competitive market (competition). Consumer Surplus being surplus from Consumer's Total Benefit (what consumers are prepared to pay for the good) minus Consumer's Total Expenditure (what consumer actually pays which is Price × Quantity). Also, Producer Surplus (profit) being Total Revenue minus Total Cost.

Word Count:

1,977 words

52

References

- Dawson, G., Mackintosh, M., Anand, P. (2006),, <u>Economics and Economic Change</u>: <u>Microeconomics</u>, Milton Keynes, The Open Univerity.

- DD202 Tutor-marked Assignments 2008 Booklet (2007) The Open University

- DD202 DVD Tutorials 5, 6, 7 and DVD Case Study 2 (2006) The Open University

- Gilbert, R. and Katz, M (2001)'An economist's guide to US v Microsoft', Journal of Economic Perspectives, vol.15, no.2, pp25-44.

- Klein, B (2001) 'The Microsoft case: what can a dominant firm do to defend its position?' Journal of Economic Perspective, vol.15, no.2 pp45-62 in Dawson, G., Mackintosh, M., Anand, P. (2006),, <u>Economics and Economic Change</u>: <u>Microeconomics</u>, Milton Keynes, The Open Univerity.

//

1a Draw a demand and supply diagram showing the effect of an increase in the supply of graduates on a typical graduate's wage.

Please refer to separate sheet attached

At Market Supply and Demand: S_L^1 (Supply of Labour) and D_L^1 (Employer's Demand for Labour), there is market equilibrium where quantity supplied equals quanity demanded. However, an increase in the Supply of Graduates to the market (other than wage rate) causes a shift in the Suppy curve right and downwards at S_L^2. This suggest that (at S_L^2 and D_L^1 market equilibrium) an increase in the Supply of Graduates <u>lowers</u> the typical Graduate's wage per hour from that offered at S_L^1 and D_L^1 market equilibrium.

1b How might the effect be modified if, at the same time, the demand for graduates increased? Would the combined effect of these changes in supply and demand raise or lower the graduate's wage?

Please refer to separate sheet attached

Both the Market Supply and Demand Curves shifts at the same time: S_L^1 (Supply of Labour) shifts Right and Downwards at S_L^2, and D_L^1 (Employer's Demand for Labour) shifts Right and Outwards at D_L^2, to reflect the increase in both the Supply and Demand for Graduates. This would (at S_L^2 and D_L^2) <u>raise the Graduate's wage</u> back up to the typical Graduate's wage offered at S_L^1 and D_L^1.

1c Comment briefly on how your analysis is related to Extracts 1 and 2.

Extract 1 says that there has been *"an equivalent shift in **employer demand** for graduates as the **supply of graduates has increased**"* so there has been *"no erosion of the graduate earnings premium"* since the 1990s when the mass expansion of higher education began. Extract 1 reflects my findings in Question 1b where an increase in both Supply and Demand causes typical Graduates's wage to remain the same and thus *"no erosion"* of typical Graduate's wage as the article puts it.

Alongside, Extract 2 notes that *"many graduates will struggle to see any financial benefit from university"*. This is because, *"any increase in tuition fees would leave many graduates unable to pay into a pension"* as they will be struggling financially to pay off the rise in tuition fees since the typical Graduate's wages offered at $S_L{}^1$ and $D_L{}^1$ (as observed in Question 1b) remains the same at $S_L{}^2$ and $D_L{}^2$ and does not reflect changes in the rising tuition fees of which tuition fees were introduced in September 2007 and is set to *"double when the fee levels are reviewed in 2010"*.

Analyse the HOUSEHOLD INCOME data with SPSS to answer question 2.

2a For each of the two regions, Inner London and Tyne & Wear, what are

- **(i) the mean (ii) the median (iii) the range, (iv) the interquartile range, and**
- **(v) the standard deviation of household incomes?**

Household Income, a Month before Interview		
	Inner London	**Tyne & Wear**
(i) Mean	3410.7997 (£3, 410.80)	2255.7705 (£2, 255.77)
(ii) Median	2802.8062 (£2, 802.81)	1608.1667 (£1, 608.17)
(iii) Range	13448.67 (£13,448.67)	10198.18 (£10, 198.18
(iv) Interquartile Range (IQR)	3225.48 (£3,225.48)	2285.36 (£2,285.36)
(v) Standard Deviation	2719.0339 (£2,719.03)	1765.4290 (£1,765.43)
( ) has been rounded up to the nearest pence		

2b Briefly describe and compare the distribution of incomes in the two regions.

The **Mean** could be defined as the total values divided by the number of values there are. The Mean for Inner London is £3, 410.80 whereas the Mean for Tyne & Wear is £2, 255.77. Immediately one can observe that the average Incomes of Households in Inner London is £1155.03 more than the average Household Incomes in Tyne & Wear.

Nonetheless, the **Median** is considered a lot more reliable than the **Mean when there is a larger spread of income values**, since the **Mean** considers all the values and proprotions them whereas the **Median** considers the middle value when all the values are placed in ascending order. When working out the Median, the middle value is obtained when the number of values gives an odd number or the two middle values divided by 2 when the number of values gives an even number. The Median for Household incomes in Inner London is £2, 802.81 and the Median Household income in Tyne & Wear is £1, 608.17. When compared with the Mean, this immediategly suggests that there are more <u>outliers</u> as observed in the **histograms (attached on a separate sheet for both regions)** for Tyne & Wear than there are for Inner London. **Outliers** are are Household income values which are abnormally high or low that can distort the ratio (proportion) of the Mean. These outliers have distorted the Mean as Tyne & Wear has a Mean which is furthest away from its Median at £647.60 compared with Inner London where there is slightly smaller £607.99 difference between its Mean and Median when compared to Tyne & Wear. This suggests that there is a greater Household income disparity (inequality) in Tyne & Wear than those Household incomes observed in Inner London.

However, the Range shows another observation. Looking at the **Range** as an Average of Measure, the Range could be obtained by subtracting the highest income value by the lowest value. Hence the Range for Household income in Inner London is given as £13,448.67 and the Range for Household income in Tyne & Wear is £10, 198.18. This findings observed from the Range suggests that although Inner London **has a higher average Household income** than that of Tyne & Wear (as discovered with the Median above), Inner London however, **has the greater Household Income inequality** than Tyne & Wear because the distance between the highest and lowest Household incomes in Inner London is greater than that of Tyne & Wear.

2c Using half median income as a measure of poverty, calculate for each region (i) the number of people living in relative poverty, and (ii) the poverty rate. Comment on the limitations, if any, of your findings for comparing poverty between the two regions.

According to Dawson et al, 'Relative' poverty line is half Median income (Average or Median Income) and is *"the income at the fifth decile:* [the income of the household] *half way along the distribution"* (Dawson et al, 2006, p253). The survey for Inner London gives 133 households. When the Household incomes are sorted into <u>ascending</u> order, the Relative Poverty line (middle value/Median) for Inner London is at the 67th Household and is at £2,802.81 average Household income.

Alongside, the survey for Tyne & Wear gives 98 households. When the Household incomes are sorted into <u>ascending</u> order, there are two middle values: the 49th and 50th Households. The Household income at the 49th Household is £1,603.33 and the Household income at the 50th Household is £1613.00. Thus the Relative Poverty line (middle Income value) is at the 49th and 50th Household and is at £1,608.17 average Household Income.

$$1603.33 + 1613.00 = 3216.33 \rightarrow \frac{3216.33}{2} = 1606.161 \rightarrow (£1,608.17)$$

Similarly, Dawson et al suggest that Poverty Rate is the number of households living below the poverty line. Hence the Poverty Rate (number of households living below the Poverty line) in Inner London living: 133 - 67 is 66 Households (living below the Poverty line). Likewise, the Poverty Rate in Tyne & Wear: 98 − 50 is 48 Households (living below the Poverty line).

From my findings for comparing poverty between the two regions, I have observed **limitations.** Inner London has 35 more households surveyed than Tyne & Wear. This limits the reliability in terms of comparing the level of poverty between Inner London and Tyne & Wear. Since equal amounts of households have not been surveyed between the two Regions Inner London and Tyne & Wear this makes it difficult to validate whether there are higher Income disparities (inequalities) in Tyne & Wear than there are in Inner London.

Alongside, the sample of households selected to be surveyed within the two regions Inner London and Tyne & Wear are relatively small compared to the number of households found in those two regions. This means that the data could be distorted as the small amount of households surveyed were selected at random and may not be a reliable reflection of the millions of households living within the regions Inner London and Tyne & Wear.

3a Construct Lorenz curves for disposable income and post-tax income using the data in Table 14 on page 15; and, with reference to the Gini coefficients for 2004/05 in Table 27 on page 16, explain what your diagram shows.

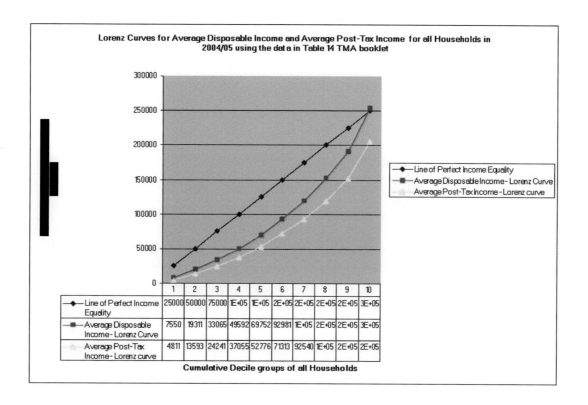

Income Inequality could be defined as disparity (unequal) distribution of income amongst the population. Similarly, **Income Distribution** is the share of Income that goes to various segments of the population.

Nonetheless, according to Dawson et al **Disposable Income** could be defined as Income after Direct taxes have been deducted - direct taxes being Income tax: *"taxes on income of people and firms"* (Dawson et al, 2006, p251). Alongside Disposable Income includes Cash Benefits (Welfare Benefits) such as *"state provided pensions and assistance for those* [on a low income and] *unable to earn an income"*. Also, from Dawson et al, **Post-Tax Inocme** could be defined as Income after both Direct taxes (Income tax) and Indirect Taxes (Value-Added-Tax/VAT on goods/purchases bought with Incomes) have been deducted.

Following on, a **Lorenz curve** is a measure of actual distribution of national income e.g. the distribution of income across all households in the population. Thus, the Lorenz Cuve expresses the relationship between cumulative percentage and and cumulative percentage of income. The bowed Lorenz Curve is looked at alongside a **Perfect Equality Line (straight**

45% line) to measure the distance apart the Lorenz Cuve is from the Perfect Equality line. Therefore, the greater the distance between the Perfect Equality Line and the Lorenz Curve, the greater the inequality of income distribution across the population.

Noting that the Lorenz Curves and Perfect Line of Equality on my diagram does not start at 0 due to the nature of the Microsoft Excel package used to construct the diagram, however this has not compromised what my diagram was designed to do. My diagram above shows that the Lorenz Cuve for Average Post-Tax Income is further away from the Stratight 45% line (Perfect Equality Line) than the Lorenz Cuve for Average Disposable Income. These findings suggest that there is more Income Inequality with Average Post-Tax Income than there are with Average Disposable Income. These results of my diagram can be compared to the **Gini Coefficients** in Table 27 (Assignment Booklet) for Disposable Income and Post-Tax Income for thesame period 2004/05 as the data used in my Diagram.

Gini Coefficient measures the degree of inequality in the distribution of national income. As a result, the Gini Coefficint looks at the ratio of income distribution for the population as a whole so that a Gini Coefficient ratio of 0 implies complete income equality across the population and a Gini Coefficient of 1 implies complete income inequality across the population. The Gini Coefficient for Disposable Income is 32% (a ratio of 0.32 or 0.3) whilst the Gini Coefficient for Post-Tax Income is 36% (a ratio of 0.36 or 0.4). Hence the Gini Coeffiient for Disposable Income is closer to 0 than the Gini Coefficient for Post-Tax Income. This means that the results for the Lorenz Curves on my diagram is reflective of the Gini Coefficients in Table 27 because the Gini Coefficients show that there are less Income disparities (inequalities) with Disposable Income than there are with Post-Tax Income.

3b To what extent is the government's redistribution of income due to benefits rather than to taxes? Use data from Tables 14 and 27 in the explanation of your answer.

Income Redistribution may be defined as the Government's welfare program to even out income disparities (unequal income) within the population to some degree. The government achieves this Redistribution of Income via Direct Taxes, Indirect Taxes, CashBenefits/Welfare Benefits (which often depends on a household's income to claim such as Jobseeker's Allowance, Incapacity/Sickness Benefit, Child Benefit and Working/Child Tax Credit) and Benefits in Kind (Universal Benefits accessible to all) such as free State Education and free National Health Service (NHS).

In Table 14, the Total Taxes (Direct and Indirect Taxes) for all households during the period 2004/06 is £11, 257. This is compared with the Total Benefits (Cash Benefits and Benefits in Kind) for all households during the same period is £9, 498. These findings immediately suggest that the Government's redistribution of income is due to Taxes. However if one looks more closely at the individual Taxes (namely Direct and Indirect Taxes) and also closely at the individual Benefits (Cash Benefits and Benefits in Kind) one can see that the Total Benefits in Kind for all households is £5,183, that is, £449 more than the total of Indirect Taxes of all Households which is at £4,734. Thus these observations suggest that Benefits in Kind being higher than Indirect Taxes are the extent to which the government's redistribution of income is due to benefits rather than to taxes

Word Count
2093 words

Appendix

Below are tables showing how the Lorenz Curves for Disposable Income and Post-tax Income have been derived.

* *Disposable Income*	*Cumulative Calculation*	Y Axis Cumaltive Disposable Income	X Axis Decile Groups of all Households
7550	7550	7550	Bottom [1]
11761	7550 + 11761 = 19311	19311	2nd [2]
13754	19311 + 13754 = 33065	33065	3rd [3]
16527	33065 + 16527 = 49592	49592	4th [4]
20160	49592 + 20160 = 69752	69752	5th [5]
23229	69752 + 23229 = 92981	92981	6th [6]
26524	92981 + 26524 = 119505	119505	7th [7]
32187	119505 + 32187 = 151692	151692	8th [8]
38875	151692 + 38875 = 190567	190567	9th [9]
63036	190567 + 63036 = 253603	253603	Top [10]

[] as shown on graph

* Average Income per household (per year) in £000's for period 2004/05

* *Average Post-Tax Income*	*Cumulative Calculation*	Y Axis Cumaltive Average Post-Tax Income	X Axis Decile Groups of all Households
4811	4811	4811	Bottom [1]
8782	4811 + 8782 = 13593	13593	2nd [2]
10648	13593 + 10648 = 24241	24241	3rd [3]
12814	24241 + 12814 = 37055	37055	4th [4]
15721	37055 + 15721 = 52776	52776	5th [5]
18537	52776 + 18537 = 71313	71313	6th [6]
21227	71313 + 21227 = 92540	92540	7th [7]
26472	92540 + 26472 = 119012	119012	8th [8]
32315	119012 + 32315 = 151332	151332	9th [9]
54937	151332 + 54937 = 206229	206229	Top [10]

[] as shown on graph

* Average Income per household (per year) in £000's for period 2004/05

References

- Dawson, G., Mackintosh, M., Anand, P. (2006),, <u>Economics and Economic Change</u>: <u>Microeconomics</u>, Milton Keynes, The Open Univerity.

- DD202 Tutor-marked Assignments 2008 Booklet (2007) The Open University

- DD202 DVD Tutorials 8 and DVD Case Study 3 (2006) The Open University

//

1a Using one diagram, show the relationship between national income and the different components of aggregate demand in a closed economy with a government sector.

Please refer to separate sheet attached

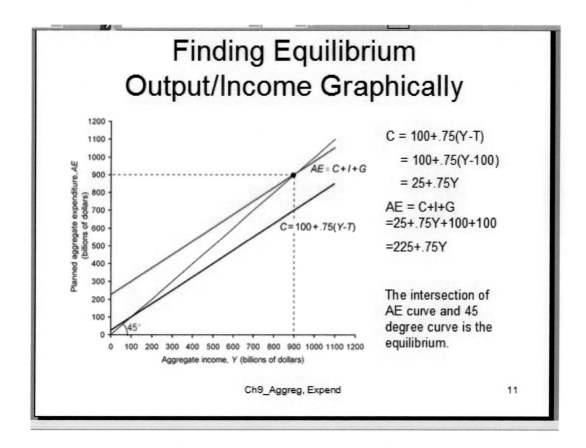

My graph shows the different components of Aggregate Demand in a closed economy with a government sector. The different components of Aggregate Demand in a closed economy with a government sector would be C + I + G (as the graph shows).

C = Consumption Demand and makes up the majority of Aggregate Expenditure and it is planned consumption of goods and services in the economy undertaken by households. Consumption Demand is also the Consumption Function $C = Co + bY_d$.

$C = Co + bY_d$ where:

C = Consumption Function

Co = Autonomous / Exogenous Consumption. Here, causes such as changes in Consumer Wealth or Consumer Confidence other than Income (Y) make up autonomous or exogenous consumption, that is consumption due to causes other than Income (Y) which causes the AD curve to shift.

b = Marginal Propensity to Consume (MPC) and is the fraction of extra income that a household consumes rather than saves. 'b' is induced consumption i.e. consumption dependent on current disposable income. The Changes to Income (Y) ceteris paribus, (other things being equal like consumer wealth except income) make up induced consumption and cause a movement along the AD curve. $0 < b < 1$ where b (MPC) is greater than 0 but less than 1 as shown below in question 2d.

Y_d = Disposable Income which is Consumption plus Saving (that are invested into i.e. shares, stocks & bonds). Disposable Income could be defined as Income after which income tax has been deducted and includes cash benefits such as welfare.

Also, C = Co + bY is <u>related to</u> the linear equation Y = MX + C or Y = C + MX, where

- C = Consumption on the Y axis
- Co = the intercept or constant on the Y axis, it always remains the same regardless of what Induced Consumption is
- b = gradient or slope
- Y = Income on the x axis and is a variable (it changes value in response to current disposable income)

The other components of Aggregate Demand in a closed economy are:

I = Firms' planned invesment on new plant and equipment and the building of new homes for households.

G = Government purchases or spending taxes it recieves (or borrowed loans it recieves) on goods and services such as welfare e.g. building roads, National Health

Service (NHS) and state-funded schools. Government also spends on subsidaries to Firms'.

My graph also shows that C + I + G equals Aggregate Demand (AD). Aggergate Demand (AD) is defined as the total of Planned Expenditure. Planned Expenditure consists of planned consumption expenditure (which depends on level of income) plus planned investment expenditure by firms which is exogenous or determined outside the model (i.e. not dependent on income), plus Government spending/purchases which also is not dependent on income since Income remains cosntant at each level of Consumption.

The graph also mentions National Income. National Income equals the sum of the incomes that all individuals in the economy earn from e.g. wages, interest, rents, and profits.

1b Carefully explain how a stock market crash which reduces people's wealth would affect aggregate demand.

A Stock could be defined as claiming partial ownership in a firm and could be sold on the margin i.e. sold using loans or part loans that are low interest which are attractive to Households (Investors). Stock market could be defined as where people buy stocks or shares in corporations / companies.

Households (Investors) purchase stocks for the reason that the stocks will increase in value (dividends) and when they sell their stocks, they will get a higher rate of return than what they originally paid for it. This gives Households confidence of increased stock of wealth. If stock prices begin to quadrupple due to more and more stocks being sold, the stock market becomes saturated (over-supplied), Households / Investors become cautious causing them to sell of their stocks which usually is sold at a lower price than what it was initally bought for and so they have less <u>wealth</u> to spend. Since, Households' wealth is eroded, Households spend less on the consumption of goods and services produced by firms and <u>save more</u>. In turn firms are unable to invest because their goods and services are consumed less by Households and in turn harms the economy because there are less injections (spending) and more leakages (saving) in the economy. Hence significantly affects Aggregate Demand by reducing it since its components, Consumption and Investment have fallen sharply. Household demand for goods and services produced by firms decrease, so firms decrease Investment. Firms decrease the production of goods and services relative to the reduced demand. Production is reduced and so workers are no longer needed so they are laid off.

These workers are now unemployed and do not have any disposable income to consume goods and services produced by firms and can only consume only <u>basic essentials,</u> this means firms are unable to invest. House prices fall and so the wealth associated with homes bought by households reduces to negative equity – living in a home worth less than their mortgage loan so that if Households decide to sell their house they are short of some of the money borrowed from lenders (such as banks/ building societies) to pay for house and so are still owing to the bank.

1c Assuming the economy was in equilibrium (at full employment) before the crash, briefly outline how the government could respond to restore that equilibrium, and the effect its policies would have.

Monetary Policy is the central bank or Bank of England's control of Money Supply or Interest Rates. After a stock market crash government could restore confidence in the economy by persuading the Bank of England (through Monetary Policy as a economic stabilizer) to cut interest rates as much as needed to restore consumer confidence and Firms' confidence in the market in order to return market / economy back to full employment equilibrium.

When interest rates are lowered, this is attractive to Households as it encourages them to <u>save less</u> and to borrow in order to consume more and thus firms's increase investment and production relative to Household Consumption.

Also, when interest rates are low, these are attractive to firms and so firms are likely to borrow money in order to invest in small projects that would create employment. The firms are able to invest because low interest rates will have little effect on their rate of return from investment.

Fiscal Policy is Government choices regarding the overall level of govertment purchases and taxes. Government (through Fiscal Policy as an economic stabilizer) could also reduce taxes and increase spending on welfare for households and subsidaries for firms. Although this would suggest that Government spending is more than Government taxes and would mean that Government would have to borrow the shortfall for taxes to deter a budget defecit. Nonetheless, less Government taxes and increased Government spending encourages households to consume since they would have more disposable income to engage in Consumption, therefore making possible for firms to invest.

1d Illustrate the effects you have analysed in 1b and 1c diagrammatically.

Please refer to separate sheets attached

Diagram 2 (question 1d part 1 regarding question 1b) suggests that a shift in Aggregate Demand (other than income) downwards due to stock market crashes significantly reduces dis-saving or borrowing and significantly increases saving as described in question 1b.

Diagram 3 (question 1d part 2 regarding question 1c) suggests that a shift in Aggregate Demand (other than income) upwards due to government intervention in the economy significantly increases dis-saving or borrowing and significantly reduces saving as described in question 1c.

2a Explain briefly what the multiplier is and why it is important, referring to your diagrams for question 1d.

The multiplier (K) is the number by which an initial increase in Aggregate Demand must be multiplied by in order to find the eventual change in National Income.

Multiplier effect assume each initial spending (i.e, each pound spent) by i.e. Household Consumption, Firms Investment Consumption and Government can raise the Aggregate Demand for Goods and Services by more than the initial amount spent and so increases National Income (as defined above in question 1a).

The formular for the Multiplier is:

$$Multiplier = \frac{1}{(1 - MPC)}$$

Alternatively,

$$Multiplier = \frac{1}{MPS}$$

A number important to the Multiplier is the marginal propensity to Consume (MPC) defined above in question 1a and as shown in Diagram 4.

The MPC is calculated as the change in consumption, ΔC, divided by the change in disposable income, ΔY_d, that is

$$MPC = MPC = \frac{\Delta C}{\Delta Yd}$$

When the Multiplier is:

$$Multiplier = \frac{1}{MPS}$$

The Marginal Propensity to save (MPS) is the fraction of a change in disposable income that a household saves rather than consumes. MPC is calculated as the change in saving, ΔS, divided by the change in disposable income, ΔY_d.

That is:

$$MPS = \frac{\Delta S}{\Delta Yd}$$

Example: If MPC = ¾ or 0.75. The Multiplier will be:

$$Multiplier = \frac{1}{1-3/4} \rightarrow \frac{1}{1-0.75} \rightarrow \frac{1}{0.25} \rightarrow 4$$

Thus, a £10 billion increase in Spending / Aggregate Demand generates £10 billion multiplied by 4 (£40 billion) increase in demand for Goods and Services (National Income), thus causes. This mulitplied effect causes the Aggregate Demand curve to shift upwards as shown in Diagram 4.

2b A new hospital is built at a cost of £200 million. If national income increases by £600 million, what is the value of the multiplier?

Assuming Multiplier is K,

Multiplier Effect = Multiplier (K)× 200million (initial spending in a component of Aggregate Demand) = 600 million

Rearranging the equation to make K the subject gives:

$$\rightarrow K \times 200 \text{ (injections, J)} = 600 \text{ (National Income, Y)}, \rightarrow K = \frac{\Delta Y}{\Delta J} \rightarrow \frac{600}{200} = 3,$$

Thus, Multiplier equals 3

2c In order to fund the Olympics, government expenditure increases by £20 billion. Using a diagram, show the final effect on national income at the existing price level if the multiplier is 3.

Please refer to separate sheet attached

2d Calculate the multipliers for:

1. **(i) country A, where the consumption function is C = 12 + 0.4Y,**

$C = C_o + bY$ where b equals 0.4 and is the Marginal Propensity to Consume (MPC) defined in question 1a above.

$$Multiplier = \frac{1}{(1-MPC)} \rightarrow \frac{1}{1-0.4} \rightarrow \frac{1}{0.6} \rightarrow 1.666666667 \_or\_ 2$$

Thus, Multiplier equals 2

2. **(ii) country B, where the marginal propensity to consume is 0.6, and**

$$Multiplier = \frac{1}{(1-MPC)} \rightarrow \frac{1}{1-0.6} \rightarrow \frac{1}{0.4} \rightarrow 2.5 \_or\_ 3$$

Thus, Multiplier equals 3

(iii) country C, where the marginal propensity to save is 0.1.

Marginal Propensity to Save (MPS) equals 0.1

$$Multiplier = \frac{1}{MPS} \rightarrow \frac{1}{0.1} \rightarrow 10$$

Thus, Multiplier equals 10

3a Discuss the view that the accelerator model of investment fails to explain important determinants of firms' investment decisions, referring to the evidence in Extract 1 and Figure 1 below.

The Accelerator Model of Investment determines the fluctuations (peaks-booms and troughs-slumps) of the course of the business cycle through fluctuations in net capital stocks.

The Accelerator model of investment as shown in Figure 1 displays an exaggerated impact of the percentage change in investment which mimicks the less exaggerated rate at which GDP growth (National Income in terms of consumer demand) increases and decreaes. Thus the Accelerator Model relates investment (production) to changes in GDP growth output (demand). The Acclerator Model asserts that a rise in GDP Growth (demand) leads firms to invest (produce) more.

Alongside Gross Investment constiutes net investment and replacement investment where, Net investment is investment which increases capital stock and Replacement investment simply maintains the existing net capital stock.

From Dawson et al, during Investment, actual capital stock K is adjusted towards desired stock K*. When K = K* net investment (gross investment minus depreciation) will cease and replacement investment will take place to keep the capital stock at desired stock K*

The Accelerator model assumes that an increase in GDP output (Demand) leads to a greater exaggerated increase in net investment

The Accelerator Model fails to explain other imporatnt determinants of firms' investment decision besides capital stock adjustment (discussed above). Such Important Investment Decisions the Accelerator Model fails to explain include (1) Interest Rates, (2) Taxes and (3) Investment Opportunites Available.

Interest Rates and taxes are very important to investment because Firms' invesment decision is planned out. Money earned through the investment of purchasing new equiptment or building homes is compared to the rate of return from the firms' investment. If high interest rates mean firms get a negative rate on their investment, then high interest rates discourages firms from investing and in turn slows down Aggregate Demand (GDP Economic Growth). As Extract 1 observes *"increases in UK interest rates"* has *"slow down"* UK economic growth.

Alongside, Government taxes such as corporate income tax and capital gains tax are also important to a firms' investment decision. This is because higher Governement taxes on investment lowers the firms rate of return from investment and so discourages firms from investing. Here, less investment injections in the economy lowers GDP.

Moreover, Available Investment Opportunities is another important determinant of firms' investment decision. Firms are reluctant to invest (and so hold money as assets / stocks or 'M-2') unless they see good investment opporunties like the 2012 Olympics which is predicted to create thousands of jobs, business and new homes sold to the competitors which would yield a higher rate of return on investment.

3b Do you agree that consumption is determined only in part by current income? Explain your answer with reference to Figures 2 and 3, and Extract 2 below.

I agree that Consumption is determined only in part by Current Income. The Marginal Propensity to Consume (MPC) related to the Consumption Function described in question 1a is induced consumption and is dependent on Disposable Income. However there are other (parts) non-income related determinants of Consumption. These include:

☐☞ Consumer Wealth;

☐☞ Consumer Expectations;

☐☞ Interest Rates when Consumers obtain credit to make their purchases (consume);

☐☞ Income distribution among househlds;

Wealth includes the consumption of cars, houses, holidays, plasma TV etc and thus when the wealth of Households rise consumption also rises as households will want to consume more (as observed in question 1b).

Consumer Expectations / Consumer Confidence are another non – income related determinatnt of consumption. When Households anticipate better times to come (such as higher income), they are likely to consume more. Similarly, referring to Figure 3, when mortgage loan rates are high, Consumer (Household) confidence are low. However, when mortgage loan rates are low, Consumer confidence increase as they anticipate better times ahead that mortgage loan rates are likely to remain low and so they make consumption e.g. they take out a mortgage loan against a house.

Interest Rates when household obtain credit are a non-income related determinant of consumption. When interest rates (APR – Annual Percentage Rates) are low Households will borrow to finance a car or to buy a house (using a mortgage loan). Likewise, as Figure 2 exposes, when the interest on money borrowed is high, Households reduce their consumption and when they are not consuming they are saving and thus saving increases and vice-versa. Moreover, MEW and Consumption Chart 1 in Extract 2 shows that when Consumer Credit (borrowing) increases, Consumption also increases and vice – versa so that *"an increase in borrowing may be an ealry indicator of consumption growth"* as the extract notes.

Distribution of Income among households is another non-income related determinant of consumption. High income households are taxed more (via Progressive taxation) in order to pay benefits to households on low incomes (redistribution of income). The income transferred to the low income households from the taxes of high income houses will be spent on consumption and the rest might be saved.

Word Count

2,105 words

References

- Dawson, G., Mackintosh, M., Anand, P. (2006),, <u>Economics and Economic Change</u>: <u>Microeconomics</u>, Milton Keynes, The Open Univerity.

- DD202 Tutor-marked Assignments 2008 Booklet (2007) The Open University

- DD202 DVD Tutorials 9 and DVD Case Study 4 (2006) The Open University

fdd202 - TMA04 AD, stock market wealth, accelerat_mod

Definitions of **Progressive Tax** on the Web:

- A tax structure where people who earn more are charged a higher percentage of their income (eg, the federal income tax).
  instech.tusd.k12.az.us/Core/glossary/ssglossary.doc
- A Tax system that takes a larger percentage from higher incomes
  www.boredofstudies.org/wiki/index.php
- http://en.wikipedia.org/wiki/Progressive_tax
  www.123exp-business.com/t/04254156580/
- A progressive tax is a tax that takes an increasing proportion of income as income rises. Income tax is an example of a progressive tax, as the ...
  www.patana.ac.th/linklearn/Linklearn_interface/results/ll_check.asp
- A taxing strategy in which tax distribution is based on the premise that higher income earners pay a higher percentage of their disposable income ...
  www.moneymatters101.com/startingabusiness/bust/bustpq.asp
- The wealthiest individuals paid at a higher rate than the less affluent.
  quizlet.com/print/221060/
- any tax in which the rate increases as the amount subject to taxation increases
  wordnet.princeton.edu/perl/webwn
- A progressive tax is a tax imposed so that the effective tax rate increases as the economic well-being increases. ...
  en.wikipedia.org/wiki/Progressive tax

Find definitions of **Progressive Tax** in: Chinese (Simplified) Chinese (Traditional) **English** all languages

Definitions of **Regressive Tax** on the Web:

- A tax that takes a larger percentage from the income of low-income people than the income of high-income people.
  investor.cisco.com/glossary.cfm
- a tax such as a sales tax that applies equally to every purchaser but which results in taking a larger percentage of income from a low-income ...
  www.wcit.org/tradeis/glossary.htm
- In an absolute sense, this is a tax in which the rate falls as the taxable base increases, as with early Social Security. ...
  www.utoledo.edu/as/pspa/faculty/LINDEEN/GLOS3260.HTM
- A tax which takes a larger percentage of lower income
  www.boredofstudies.org/wiki/index.php
- A regressive tax is a tax imposed so that the effective tax rate decreases as the amount to which the rate is applied increases. ...
  en.wikipedia.org/wiki/Regressive tax

83

- A tax structure where people who earn more pay a smaller percentage of their income in taxes (eg, sales taxes).
  instech.tusd.k12.az.us/Core/glossary/ssglossary.doc

Find definitions of **Regressive Tax** in: Chinese (Simplified) Chinese (Traditional) **English** all languages

//

Find definitions of **Regressive Tax** in: Chinese (Simplified) Chinese (Traditional) **English** all languages

1a Which country in Table 1 below will export Machines to the other?

Opportunity Cost is the value of the next best alternative product that a nation such as Ghana or Israel could have produced. Hence it measures what Ghana or Israel gave up in producing the most preferred good.

Similarly, Comparative Advantage arises for a nation such as Ghana when its opportunity cost of producing a good is lower than that of another nation such as Israel. Thus Comparative Advantage indicates which goods nations such as Ghana should export or import.

Likewise, Specialisation suggests that nations such as Ghana or Israel should maximise production by producing goods that is most cost-effective (or cheaper) for them produce.

As a result, Israel should 'specialise' in exporting Machines to Ghana because if Israel gives up 2 tonnes of Cocoa, it can produce 1 Machine. Israel has a lower opportunity cost of producing Machines relative to producing Cocoa, where the opportunity cost of producing 1 Machine is 2 tonnes of Cocoa. However, Ghana has a high opportunity cost of producing Machines relative to producing Cocoa, where the opportunity cost of producing 1 Machine is 5 tonnes of Cocoa. Therefore Ghana would lose out if it decides to specialise in producing Machines because it is much cheaper for Ghana to produce Cocoa than it is for them produce Machines since Ghana produces 5 times more Cocoa than Machines. Ghana is much more efficient at producing Cocoa than they are at producing Machines.

1b Would trade occur if the (world) price of 1 Machine were 6 tonnes of cocoa?

Comparative Advantage suggests that it is always better to trade than not to trade because Comparative Advantage indicates which goods are cheaper to import or export than to produce solely for one's own nation which is not cost-efficient or productive. For Israel, the cost of producing 1 Machine is 2 tonnes of Cocoa, whereas in Ghana, the cost of producing 1 Machine is 5 tonnes of Cocoa.

As established in **question 1a,** Israel is more efficient if Israel specialise in producing Machines whereas Ghana is more efficient if Ghana specialises in producing Cocoa. Previously, Ghana got 1 Machine for exporting 5 tonnes of Cocoa. Now that the world price of 1 Machine is 6 tonnes of Cocoa, Ghana would now have to export 6 tonnes (1 tonne more) of Cocoa for just 1 Machine. This implies that the world price of Cocoa has fallen relative to 1 Machine, because Ghana are now having to export 1 tonne more of Cocoa for just 1 Machine. Thus, Ghana would gain less revenue for their Cocoa where as Israel will gain more because they would now get 1 tonne more of Cocoa (from 5 tonnes to 6 tonnes) for exporting just 1 Machine to Ghana.

Hence despite Ghana's 'trade deterioration' with falling World prices of Cocoa, Ghana are *"better off still trading than not trading"* (Dawson et al, 2006, p406)

1c Which country would <u>gain more</u> if 1 Machine is traded for 4 tonnes of cocoa? Carefully explain all your answers. (15%)

Gains of trade refer to the benefits of extra production and consumption that can be achieved through international trade.

Israel has an opportunity cost ratio of 1 Machine for 2 tonnes of Cocoa. Ghana has an opportunity cost ratio of 1 Machine for 5 tonnes of Cocoa.

As established in **question 1a**, Ghana is better off maximising their production by specialising in producing Cocoa because they can produce five times more Cocoa than Machines and would lose out if they decided to give up producing Cocoa for Machines. Similarly, in this circumstance, Israel are better off maximising their production by producing Machines because Ghana is better off at producing Cocoa more cheaply than Israel.

Thus if Ghana was to specialise in producing Cocoa and Israel was to specialise in producing Machines, Israel now gains less Cocoa than before. Israel gains less because previously as in **question 1a**, Israel got 5 tonnes of Cocoa in return for trading 1 Machine. Now Israel gets 4 tonnes (1 tonne less) of Cocoa in return for trading 1 Machine. As a result, Ghana gains more.

Ghana gains more because previously in **question 1a**, Ghana gave up 5 tonnes (1 tonne more) of Cocoa in return for 1 Machine. Now Ghana gives up less Cocoa for the same 1 Machine, for instance Ghana gives up 4 tonnes (1 tonne less) of Cocoa for 1 Machine.

2a Using Tables 3 and 4, calculate Israel's terms of trade for 2004, 2005 and 2006.

Terms of Trade measures relative prices where the ratio of the Price of a Country (i.e. Israel) is relative to the Country's (Israel) prices of Imports. Hence it measures the number of units of Imports that can be exchanged for a unit of export.

The Formula for working out Terms of Trade (the Terms of Trade Index) is:

Terms of Trade Index = $\dfrac{Export\_Price\_Index}{Import\_Price\_Index} \cdot 100$

or

Terms of Trade Index = $\dfrac{Export\_Price\_Index}{Import\_Price\_Index} \times 100$

2004 Total Imports = 111.8, 2004 Total Exports = 107.4

Terms of Trade Index $\rightarrow \dfrac{107.4}{111.8} \times 100 = 96.06440072$ or 96.1 (percentage price ratio)

2005 Total Imports = 120.0, 2005 Total Export = 116.2

Terms of Trade Index $\rightarrow \dfrac{116.2}{120.0} \times 100 = 96.83333333$ or 97 (percentage price ratio)

2006 Total Imports = 127.1, 2006 Total Exports = 121.1

Terms of Trade Index $\rightarrow \dfrac{121.1}{127.1} \times 100 = 95.27930763$ or 95 (percentage price ratio)

2b Which price movements have most influenced its terms of trade since 2004? (15%)

Balance of Payment (BoP) is a country's trade and financial transaction (for both visibles i.e. goods and invisibles i.e. services) with the rest of the world over a period of time. Whereas, Balance of Trade is a statement of only a country's visible goods (omitting invisibles, such as services) over a period of time.

Trade Surplus occurs when a nation's exports of goods and services are more than its imports. Likewise, Trade Deficit occurs when a nation's imports are more than its exports, thus such nation would have to borrow from abroad to make up the shortfall for too much imports exceeding exports.

Price Movement refers to the Changes in the <u>Terms of Trade Price Ratios</u> from one year to the next, i.e. in 2004, 2005 and 2006.

A percentage price ratio of 100 or more is desirable (in terms of exports) because it would indicate that for a percentage price ratio of 100, there is relatively little difference between Export prices relative to Imports prices, thus Terms of Trade are good. However, a percentage price ratio of more than 100 would indicate that Export prices is more than Import prices and so Terms of Trade is even better (i.e. has trade surplus / balance of trade surplus).

The Aggregate Components of an Open Economy are Consumption Household Demand <u>plus</u> Investing Firms' Demand <u>plus</u> Government Purchases <u>plus</u> (Export <u>minus</u> Imports). Also Imports (import expenditure) represent leakages/withdrawals (money flows out) in an Open Economy such as Israel's' while Exports (export expenditure) represents Injections (money flows into) an Open Economy. Thus, Exports being more than Imports would suggest an Economy is experiencing Economic Growth.

Nonetheless, from 2004 to 2006, the Terms of Trade Percentage Price ratios for Israel have given a **Trade Deficit (Balance of Trade Deficit)** because the Terms of Trade Percentage Price ratios have been less than 100 indicating that Import prices are more than Export prices **(as observed in question 2a)**

However, the price movements that have most influenced Israel's terms of trade since 2004 are those for 2004 (96.1) and 2004 (97) **outlined in question 2a.** This is because they are closer to 100 indicating that there is relatively little difference between Import and Export prices, thus trade deficit are not significant, because a fall in export prices makes it attractive to foreign importers abroad as goods would be bought cheaply and in turn would improve the Balance of Payment.

3a According to Extracts 1 and 2 below, what causes Ghana's terms-of-trade difficulties?

World prices dictate the price of goods Ghana exports as noted in Extract 1. Thus Terms of Trade fluctuations (upswings and downturns) are exogenous (outside Ghana's control). Hence a slump/decline in the World price for Cocoa as Extract 2 notes, *"halving of world price of Cocoa"* would cause Terms-of-Trade difficulties for Ghana because it would cause Ghana's terms of Trade to fall, since Ghana will be making less revenue for producing the same amount of Cocoa before the world price of Cocoa slump. Ghana's terms of trade have fallen due to oversupply of Cocoa exports. As Extract 1 notes, developing countries such as Ghana rely heavily on commodity exports whose prices are volatile due to the forces of supply and demand. Similarly Extract 2 notes, there is an over-supply of Cocoa since Cocoa *"overwhelmingly accounts for most exports"*. Thus an over-supply of Cocoa or too much world supply of Cocoa in relation to less demand causes the World price of Cocoa to fall.

3b Draw a diagram showing the supply and demand for cedi, and, assuming exchange rates are flexible, explain how the equilibrium exchange rate (expressed as $/cedi) is determined. Then, using two other diagrams, explain the effect on the exchange rate of (i) a rise in import prices, and (ii) a fall in export prices.

Flexible or floating exchange rates adjust automatically to change (automatically adjusts its balance of payments) because its equilibrium (where supply equals demand) exchange rate is <u>determined</u> by the market forces of supply and demand unlike fixed exchange rates which are determined / fixed by the Central Bank / government. In other words, it is determined through the interaction of buyers and sellers of currencies in the market.

(i) A rise in import prices (other than exchange rate) reduces demand for the currency Cedis and causes the Demand Curve to shift left and downwards. The Demand for a Cedi currency is carried out by foreign United States importers/residents. Import prices rises because as the demand for Cedis increases, the price of Cedis will appreciate (the value of Cedis will increase) meaning that more United States (US) dollars are required to purchase or import fewer Cedis. Thus the exchange rate between United States Dollars and Ghana Cedis decreases (i.e. the value of Cedis / importing Cedis rises) making importing Cedis less attractive to US foreign residents and so the demand of Cedis by US foreign residents decreases. Hence as Import increases demand decreases so the Demand Curve slopes down to reflect this.

(ii) A fall in export prices (other than exchange rate) increases the supply for cedes and causes the Supply Curve to shift right and downwards. The supply of a currency is carried out through domestic exports i.e. through Ghana's domestic residents. United States foreign residents demand Cedis by selling dollars on the foreign exchange market i.e. through banks or bureau de change. If the exchange rate between United States dollars and Ghana Cedis is high i.e. if the price of Cedis falls / depreciates (the value of Cedis is low), this is attractive to United States foreign residents, so the demand for Cedis by US foreign residents will increase as more Cedis will be purchased using fewer dollars. Thus Ghana would have to export / supply more Cedis to meet with US demand. Hence a fall in export prices increases the exchange rate as more Cedis will be supplied to the United States for fewer dollars and so the Supply curve slopes upwards to reflect this.

<u>For diagrams, please refer to separate sheets attached.</u>

3c Explain the argument for the view that developing countries subject to terms of trade shocks should not adopt a fixed exchange rate. Illustrate your explanation with reference to Ghana. (35%)

Fixed exchange rates pegs (fixes) are good for developing countries with small trade as they can peg their currency to countries with large trade i.e. developed countries. A scenario for instance, if the Exchange rate for Ghana's Cedis to US dollars was 10 Cedis to 1 Dollar, 10 Cedis would be fixed to 1 dollar. The fixed rate would be 1 Dollar divided by 10 Cedis which equals 0.10 and this fix rate is fixed by Central Bank through government policies and remains the same for international trade. However problems arise for developing countries such as Ghana when they peg their currency to a developed country's currency such as United States dollars. The problem here is that as the (Dollar) currency of the developed country (United States) appreciates (increases in value), the developing Country's (Ghana) Cedi currency also appreciates. Thus an appreciation of currency would not be good for trade Exports as it would mean Ghana's exports become more expensive for Importers in the United States as United States Importers would now require more Dollars to purchase fewer goods or expensive goods from Ghana. Thus demand from the United States will decrease causing Imports into Ghana to rise faster than exports. This results in terms-of-trade shock as Ghana's Balance of Payment has deteriorated since Imports would be more than Exports. Thus, this terms-of-trade shock would indicate that the Ghanaian government would have to devalue Ghana's appreciating currency through sterilisation so that Ghana's currency decreases in value, making Ghana's export cheaper to purchase for fewer dollars by US foreign residents

In conclusion, developing countries subject to terms of trade shocks should not adopt a fixed exchange rate because it would cause their currency to appreciate (increase in value) which is not good for Exports as Ghana's exported goods becomes expensive for the importing United States country as the United States (US) would require more money to purchase few goods from Ghana.

4 What, according to the WTO, is the main policy instrument used by Ghana to achieve economic growth? Carefully explain the problems this policy may cause. (35%)

The World Trade Organisation (WTO) is an international organisation established in 1995 and replaced its predecessor: the General Agreement on Tariff and Trade (GATT). Unlike GATT which was set up in 1948 to promote free trade, the WTO would administer and implement multi-lateral (cross) trade agreements, reviewing trade policies and working in partnership with other international institutions regarding global economic policy making.

Nonetheless, according to Extract 2, the WTO (World Trade Organisation) notes that the main policy instrument used by Ghana to achieve economic growth is Tariff (Import Tariff).

A Tariff works by imposing tax on imported goods or imports. Most of the cost of import tax (tariff) comes from Domestic Consumers which the Domestic Government receives. Although tax / tariff on imported goods reduce imports, imports will not fall much and the Domestic Government will receive some revenue from the imported goods in the form of tariff (import taxes). Similarly, Import Tariff will be effective in reducing Imports if Ghana's demand for imported goods decrease due to a depreciation in Ghana's Cedi currency (price of Cedi currency falls) making Imports into Ghana expensive and less desirable to Ghana's Consumers and at the same time making Ghana's exports cheaper and more desirable to foreign Importers / Consumers.

However, when taking into consideration Comparative Trade (Comparative Advantage) the trade policy (import tariff) can cause problems for Ghana's economy because import tariff can reduce the level of trade into Ghana such as goods which are cheaper for Ghana to import (such as Machines as in **question 1a**) than to produce. Here, the Comparative Advantage of Ghana importing goods would mean it would release the burden of Ghana trying to i.e. specialise in both Cocoa and Machine which would means less production. However, Ghana can maximise their production by importing goods that have a high opportunity cost (are more expensive) for Ghana to produce and focusing their production on goods that they are specialist at producing more cheaply for exports of which Ghana's cheaper price of exporting goods would attract a high demand from foreign Importers who wish to purchase (import) Ghana's cheap goods using less currency.

To conclude, although Ghana recognises import tariff policy instrument as their main instrument to achieving economic growth, the disadvantage to this policy instrument is that it can reduce imports which are essential for the comparative advantage of trading with other nations.

Word Count

2, 011 words

References

- Dawson, G., Mackintosh, M., Anand, P. (2006),, <u>Economics and Economic Change</u>: <u>Microeconomics</u>, Milton Keynes, The Open Univerity.

- DD202 Tutor-marked Assignments 2008 Booklet (2007) The Open University

- DD202 DVD Tutorials 10 and 11 and DVD Case Study 5 (2006) The Open University

dd202 - TMA05 int'l trade, int'l finance

//

Investment is carried out by Firms and is Firms' planned invesment on new plant and equipment and the building of new homes for households.

The *inflation rate* is the percentage change in the the level of prices and Inflation is caused by rising economic growth. If inflation increases, it can cause problems. For example, rising inflation causes firms to make pessimistic forecasts of increased costs and low revenue (lower return on investment) which discourages them from investing. Similarly, high inflation causes the Bank of England through monetary policy to increase interest rates which in turn reduces Consumption and Investment. A reduction in Consumption and Investment could reduce inflation but at the same time could reduce the rate of economic growth since fewer goods and being produced (and exported). Also inflation causes workers to negoitiate wage increases as they realise the impact of increases in price of goods (due to inflation) which reduces the amount of goods their money can buy (i.e. reduces the purchasing power of their income / money). However increasing wage rates would make employers pass their increasing costs (wage increases) into higher prices of goods purchased by the workers (consumers).

Economic Growth referes to the ability for individuals to enjoy better living standards through a rise in the number of people employed (**higher employment**) which encourages more consumption in goods and services that encourages firms to increase demand and output (**Investment Accelerator Effect**). More consumption encourages investment in new capital machinery that could help to sustain economic growth. Economic growth also refers to increases in Gross Domestic Product (GDP) which GDP is the total value of goods and services produced within by a nation.

1a What were the statistical associations in the UK from 1991 to 2006 between (i) interest rates and inflation, and (ii) inflation and investment?

1b Describe the differences between (i) the direction and (ii) the strength of these associations.

My scatterplots show the statistical associations/relationship in the UK from 1991 to 2006 between interest rates and inflation, and inflation and investment. For example, my observation of the scatterplot 1 shows that the association between interest and inflation has a <u>weak positive (direction) correlation/relationship</u>. Also the scatterplot for interest rates and inflation shows that there are more changes between interest rates and inflation because the dots are quite dispersed as supported by its regression of 45.729 (45.73). Additionally, the R squared for the scatterplot interest rates and inflation gives an indication of how well the regression line fits the data. The R squared has a high variance of 0.728 (0.73 or 73%). This suggests that 73% out of 100% of the variance in the dependent variable Interest rates on the y axis can be explained by the changes in the independent variable inflation on the x axis, and that changes in the value of interest rates correspond to changes in the value of inflation on the regression line. The remaining 27% of the variation of interest rates are not accounted for by the regression line. Thus the R squared variance of 73% suggests that the regression line fits the data quite well.

Alongside, observations of my second scatterplot shows that the association between inflation and investment has a <u>weak negative (direction) correlation</u>. This scatterplot shows that there are less changes between inflation and investment since the dots are quite clustered together as supported by its regression of 18.854 (18.85). In addition, the inflation and investment scatterplot gives a low R squared variance of 0.476 (0.48 or 48%). This R squared variance suggests that 52% of the the variation Inflation (dependent variable on y axis) are not accounted by the regression line and 52% being a larger value than the R squared variance indicates that the regression line does not fit the data very well.

1c **According to the statistical association you have found, by how much would the rate of interest rise if the inflation rate rose by 2 per cent? Does your answer show that the Bank of England followed a very simple rule to decide the level of interest rates? (40%)**

Linear Equation is **y = a + bx**

According to the Coefficient I found from the Linear Regression of Interest Rate and Inflation:

		Unstandardized Coefficients	
Coefficients (a)			
Model		**B**	Std. Error
1	(Constant)	3.657	.485
	Inflation	1.074	.175

The Regression Line is the Linear Equation and this is **y = a + bx,** where:

y = the dependent variable and is Interest Rate

a = the y Intercept or constant, its value is (3.657 as above in the Coefficient Table produced from the Linear Regression)

b = the gradient or slope and its value is 1.074 (from the Coefficient - Table above)

x = the independent variable and is Inflation and the <u>question 1c</u> notes that the value for this is 2 (2%)

Thus,   →   y = a + bx

- Interest Rate = 3.657 + (1.074 × 2)

- Interest Rate = 3.657 + (2.148)

- Interest Rate = 5.805 (or 5.8%)

Hence, the rate of interest would rise by 5.8 per cent if the inflation rate rose by 2 per cent

My calculation above shows that the Bank of England followed a very simple rule to decide the level of interest rates.

2 Briefly describe, and account for, the differences between the CPI and the RPI between 1994 and 2003 shown in Extract 1 and Figure 1 below. What are their relative merits as measures of inflation? (20%)

CPI (Consumer Price Index) and Retail Price Index are used for macroeconomic purposes and with the use of a Price Index, CPI and RPI both measure the average change from month to month in the price of consumer goods and services purchased in the UK. There is a difference between CPI and RPI.

According to Extract 1, this difference is in the basket of *"goods, services, population"* it covers and *"method of calculation"*. For instance, the CPI basket includes some items that represent costs to foreign visitors to the UK and also residents of all households which are excluded from the RPI.

However, the RPI basket includes average spending pattern of the great majority of private households in the UK of which these exclude some private households such as pensioner and high-income households *("the richest 4 per cent of the population"* that can distort the spending pattern of average households) – a contrast to CPI which CPI represents costs of all households. Also, the RPI includes items representing owner-occupying housing costs including mortgage interest payments costs (*'mortgage repayments'* costs), *'depreciation'* costs and *'council tax'* costs which are excluded from the CPI.

Alongside, from my observation of Figure 1 from the Period 1994 to 2003, there appears to be striking differences between the percentage change in CPI Inflation and RPI Inflation. Initially, it appears from 1994 to 1995 both the percentage change in CPI Inflation and RPI Inflation fell and rose together. However from the fourth quarter of 1995 the percentage change in CPI Inflation rose above 3.6% while the percentage change for RPI Inflation had fallen to just above 2%. Alongside in first quarter of 1997, the percentage change of RPI Inflation and CPI Inflation where both equivalent at 2.6%, however after this the percentage change in CPI Inflation appeared to be falling while the percentage change in RPI Inflation appeared to have risen until the first quarter of 1998 but fell sharply after this until the third quarter of 1993 and then rose again sharply. Although during the third quarter of 2001 and the fourth quarter of 2002 the percentage changes in CPI were higher than that of RPI Inflation, the percentage change in CPI inflation remained low from there while the percentage change in RPI Inflation had risen sharply to almost 2.4 %.

The relative merits of CPI Inflation and RPI inflation as measures of inflation is that RPI is more volatile as percentage changes in RPI Inflation rise or fall sharply compared to that of CPI Inflation. The percentage changes in CPI inflation fall or rise gradually but have generally remained low compared with RPI Inflation. With this at the fact that the RPI includes items (not included in CPI Inflation) representing owner-occupying housing costs (i.e. mortgage repayments and depreciation and council tax) which are very responsive to Inflation helps to explain why *"in 2003 the UK government adopted the CPI as the official measure of inflation in setting the Bank of England the task of keeping CPI inflation"* at 2%.

3a   How did the analysis of the Phillips curve lead policy makers to concentrate on the control of inflation?

The *Phillips Curve* shows the relationship between the inflation rate and the unemployment rate. The original Phillips curve by Professor A.W. Phillips in 1958 assumes that there is a trade-off between inflation and unemployment. To lower inflation rate would mean accepting a higher rate of unemployment. This was the case in the in the 1960s and early 1970s as inflation appeared to respond to this trade-off in the Short-run. A trade-off between inflation and unemployment meant that policy makers will be unable to simultaneously achieve both low inflation and low unemployment but however policy makers could settle for particular levels of unemployment and inflation they regard as the best compromise for the economy.

Nonetheless, the arguments (for original Phillips Curve in short-run) for the trade-off or inverse / negative relationship between inflation and unemployment were that as unemployment falls (and employment increases), wage inflation (and price inflation or changes in the level of prices of goods and services) increases. The demand for labour by employers increases, and puts pressure on employers to offer higher levels of pay in order to recruit and retain their key workers. Also, falling unemployment causes an increase in employment which leads to increase in Aggregate Demand, in turn which could lead to 'demand-pull inflation' whereby more money is needed to purchase few goods, ['demand-pull inflation' is inflation caused by excessive increase in (aggregate) demand unlike 'cost-push inflation' caused by firms increases in cost from wage increases and government taxes which could push up firms prices to cover firm's increasing costs and cause a decrease in aggregate supply (left shift)].

However and according to Friedman, (in the Long-run) by the 1970s and 1980s, the Phillips Curve had broken down since it appeared to show no relationship or correlation between the rate of inflation and the rate of unemployment. <u>Here, high inflation and high unemployment tended to co-exist</u> (known as <u>stagflation</u>). Friedman argued that In the <u>long run</u>, the the Phillips Curve was vertical as it moved back to the natural rate of unemployment (the level of voluntary unemployment when the labour market is in equilibrium, the rate of unemploy which is not possible to reduce below this rate without increasing the rate of inflation). This had implications for policy because in the 1960s and early 1970s the government was commited to maintaining full employment but attempts to reduce unemployment below its natural rate would be inflationary since it would cause price levels (inflation) to increase, and hence led policy makers since the mid-1970s to control this inflation rather than reducing unemployment below its natural rate. This analysis of the effect of <u>expansionary</u> macroeconomic policy is called the Friedman expectations-augmented Phillips Curve analysis (see Appendix 2).

3b Identify the main macroeconomic variables considered at the Monetary Policy Committee's meeting in November 2006 (Extract 2), and explain the economic analysis and evidence underlying the decision to raise Bank Rate (40%).

Macroeconomic variables are variables which are considered important when studying macroeconomics (i.e. the economy as a whole). Such macroeconomic variables include inflation, interest rates (demand side), unemployment and employment (supply side).

Economic Analysis is anlysis undertaken using economic values.

The main macroeconomic variables considered by the Monetary Policy Committee's meeting in November 2006 (in Extract 2) are interest rates, GDP Growth (Economic Growth), CPI Inflation (Consumer Price Index Inflation), unemployment and employment.

Extract 2 notes that the risks of CPI inflation exceeding 2% inflation target in the medium-term would emerge if Bank rate / interest rates remained at 4.75% (as it would increase borrowing of bank loans from Frims causing them to invest more and also increase borrowing of bank loans from households causing them to consume more leading to economic growth on the Aggregate demand side). Thus, for those members of the committee concerned about this risk, "*an immediate increase of 0.25 percentage points in Bank Rate* [interest rates]" would be necessary to bring inflation in line with target set for inflation (which is 2%). According to economic theory, by increasing interest rates would affect Aggregate demand side economics, as it would reduce borrowing of bank loans by firms leading to less investment in small project that would bring about more jobs and workers needed to cope with the demand of the jobs and could see reduced investment injections into the economy (reduced economic growth). Also it would reduce borrowing of bank loans by Consumers would mean less consumption and thus less injections into the economy (reduced economic growth).

However, *Labour supply* is the amount of labour that households want to supply at each given wage rate. While labour demand *is* the amount of labour that firms want to employ at each given wage rate

Likewise, Structural unemployment unemployment is changes in the structure of the economy that result in a significant loss of jobs in some industries.

Fiscal Policy is Government choices regarding the overall level of government purchases and taxes.

Following, for *"one member.....[t]he key uncerntainty was on the supply side* [economics]. Extract 2 notes it is believed that *"the rise in unemployment had in part been caused by relatively weak demand for labour....[due to] downward pressure of wages* [low wages] i.e. According to the Supply and Demand law of Labour or original Phillips Curve hypothesis, when labour demand decreases, the equilibrium wage will fall. Also, according to supply side economics high rates of taxes reduce individuals' incentive to work (which could be avoided by increasing Aggregate Supply i.e cutting tax rates would encourage individuals to find work). By increasing output in Aggregate Supply (i.e. cutting tax rates to expand labour supply) would increase the productivity of the economy (reduce unemployment to increase employment) and thereby help to reduce the risk of a 'rise in (structural unemployment) which can reduce economic growth. Similarly Government spending on education and training improves workers' human capital as workers will be able to keep their jobs when new knowledge-based information is introduced into their job roles.

Anticipated Inflation or Expected Inflation occurs when individuals correctly factor in expected changes in inflation into their negoitiations for wage increases, while unanticipated inflation is changes in inflation are not factored into (considered in) negoitiations for higher wages and so can lead employers to cut jobs to reduce costs.

Alongside, Extract 2 also notes that there was a risk of *"expected inflation....* feeding into higher *wages during the coming wage round by raising* [interest] *rates* [against the risk of inflation] would only make the economy volatile rather than set inflation target at 2% as needed. Here higher wages are eroded because of higher prices (inflation)

Also Extract 2 notes: Inflation expectations according to the surveys were flat or falling and so prospective wage growth [that could push up inflation from question 3a] was likely to be muted [stagnant/stanted].

From question 3a attempts to reduce unemployment below its natural rate would be inflationary since it would cause price levels (inflation) to increase, and hence led policy makers since the mid 1970s to control this inflation rather than reducing unemployment below its natural rate. This is the evidence underpinning the desion to raise Bank Rate (interest rate)

Word Count
2,012 words

Scatterplot 1: Interest Rates and Inflation

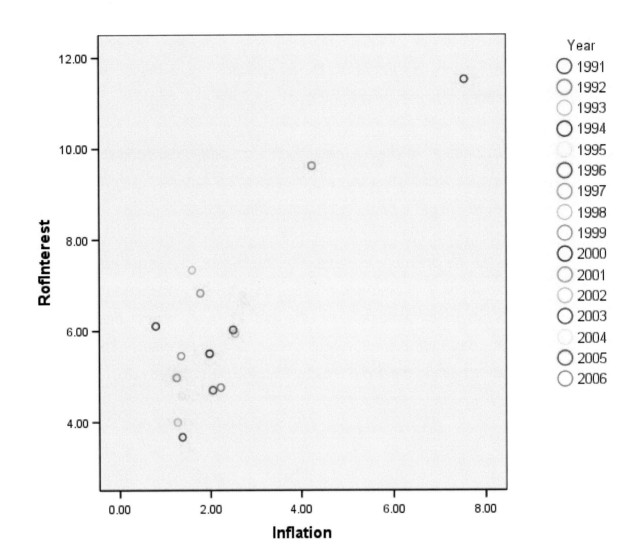

Regression

Variables Entered/Removed(b)

Model	Variables Entered	Variables Removed	Method
1	Inflation(a)	.	Enter

a All requested variables entered.
b Dependent Variable: RofInterest

Model Summary

Model	R	R Square	Adjusted R Square	Std. Error of the Estimate
1	.854(a)	.728	.709	1.10340

a Predictors: (Constant), Inflation

ANOVA(b)

Model		Sum of Squares	df	Mean Square	F	Sig.
1	Regression	45.729	1	45.729	37.560	.000(a)
	Residual	17.045	14	1.217		
	Total	62.774	15			

a Predictors: (Constant), Inflation
b Dependent Variable: RofInterest

Coefficients(a)

Model		Unstandardized Coefficients		Standardized Coefficients	t	Sig.
		B	Std. Error	Beta		
1	(Constant)	3.657	.485		7.536	.000
	Inflation	1.074	.175	.854	6.129	.000

a Dependent Variable: RofInterest

+++

+++++

Scatterplot 2: Inflation and Investment

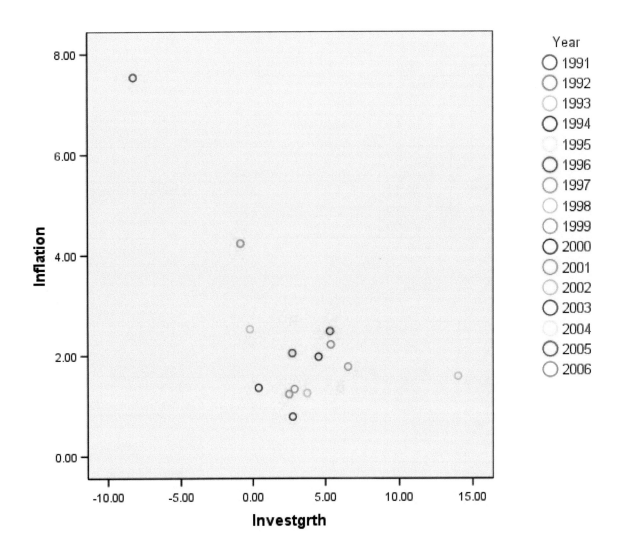

Regression

Variables Entered/Removed(b)

Model	Variables Entered	Variables Removed	Method
1	Investgrth(a)	.	Enter

a All requested variables entered.
b Dependent Variable: Inflation

Model Summary

Model	R	R Square	Adjusted R Square	Std. Error of the Estimate
1	.690(a)	.476	.438	1.21854

a Predictors: (Constant), Investgrth

ANOVA(b)

Model		Sum of Squares	df	Mean Square	F	Sig.
1	Regression	18.854	1	18.854	12.697	.003(a)
	Residual	20.788	14	1.485		
	Total	39.642	15			

a Predictors: (Constant), Investgrth
b Dependent Variable: Inflation

Coefficients(a)

Model		Unstandardized Coefficients		Standardized Coefficients		
		B	Std. Error	Beta	t	Sig.
1	(Constant)	3.045	.373		8.165	.000
	Investgrth	-.245	.069	-.690	-3.563	.003

a Dependent Variable: Inflation

+++

+++++

113

Longrun Augmented Phillips Curve

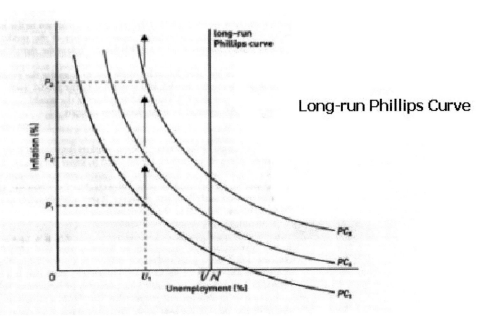

Long-run Phillips Curve

U$_1$ attempts to reduce unemployment
at this level would increase inflation

U$_n$ natural rate of unemployment

P = prices

+++
++++

114

References

1. Dawson, G., Mackintosh, M., Anand, P. (2006),, <u>Economics and Economic Change</u>: <u>Microeconomics</u>, Milton Keynes, The Open Univerity.

2. DD202 Tutor-marked Assignments 2008 Booklet (2007) The Open University

3. DD202 DVD Tutorials 12 and 13 (2006) The Open University

//..//

PART A – RESEARCH METHODS, LAW

PART B – MATHS, SCIENCE PROJECT EXAMPLES

PART B – eBUSINESS PROJECT REPORT EXAMPLE, MONOPOLY MARKET AND COMPETITIVE ENTRY EXPLAINED - SEMIOTICS, TEXTUAL ANALYSIS - BELL/CASTELLS 'INFORMATION SOCIETY' ON 'WORK'- MEDIA POLICY, SOCIAL JUSTICE SOCIAL POLICY, CRIME AND JUSTICE, CRIMINOLOGY, EBUSINESS ECONOMICS

PART A

- Validity (the degree to which the research study results supports the intended conclusion.
- Reliability (the idea that under specific conditions, the research study results fits the time and purpose for which it was designed
- .Comprehensiveness (the research study results shows connections among issues e.g.social services, education and training, economic development and housing
- Coherence (the requirement for the research study results to 'fit' pre-exisiting believes

LAW, WHAT IS LAW, CONTROLLING BEHAVIOURS, CREATING FAIRNESS FREEDOMS, INDIVIDUAL AND THE STATE, CASE LAW CREATED BY JUDGES, ACTS OF PARLIAMENT / LEGISLATION CREATED BY GOVERNMENT, COURTS OF HUMAN RIGHTS ANOTHER BODY OF LAW, TORT LAW CORRECTING WRONGFUL ACT THROUGH COMPENSATION PERSONAL INJURY INSURANCE, RULE OF LAW AV DICEY.

PART B

MATHS – SIMULTANEOUS EQUATIONS, SCIENCE INVESTIGATION: RATE OF REACTION

PART C

POLICY AND THE SOCIAL SCIENCES AND LITERATURE

MEDIA POLICY

TEXTUAL ANALYSIS – DENOTATION, CONNOTATION, SIGNIFIER, SIGNIFIED, SEMIOTICS

BELL / CASTELLS 'INFORMATION SOCIETY' ON 'WORK' Outline Bell's and Castells' research on the 'information society'. What would you need to consider in evaluating their research? Answer 'Work'

SOCIAL JUSTICE, CRIME JUSTICE, SOCIAL POLICY, CRIMINOLOGY

ECONOMICS - PARETO EFFICIENT MARKET IS COMPETITVE MARKET ,

- ASSYMETRIC INFORMATION AND HOW YOU SORT 'LEMON' CAR INFORMATION, STARTING POINT ALL SECOND HAND CARS ARE LEMON
- ENGLISH LITER

CARS NO WAY OF TELLING CAR WORKS UNLESS TAKE IT HOME AND TEST IT OUT - PROJECT **Topic Title: Determinants of Wage Biases in the UK Labour Market**

CONTENTS PAGE

11 - APPENDICES
APPENDIX 1: TABLE OF RESULTS
APPENDIX 2: SYMBOLS USED

For the Purposes of the Quantitative Analysis Project regarding Wage Discrimination and Wage Differentials, during my period at Residential School at the University of Bath, I obtained a set of Econometric Results. Econometrics is the application of statistics to study economic data, in this case Wage Discrimination and Wage Differentials. The Econometric Results was obtained using Dummy Variables (where Dummy Variables in a regression model have two categories, valued zero and 1, where e.g. male = 0 and female = 1). The Econometric Results is also based on the Ordinary Least Square (OLS) Linear Regression which is a technique used for estimating the unknown parameters (relationship between e.g. dependent γ Variable Wages and independent χ Variable Region etc) in a linear regression model by employing formals such as adjusted R squared (R^2) and P-Value etc. My Econometric Results uses Multiple Regression (defined below) for the basis of looking at number of casual factors (independent χ Variables) such as Employment, being Female etc., to test for any relationship with the dependent γ Variable Wages, in order to find any evidence to support the Alternative Hypothesis of Wage Differentials or in the extreme case, if the strength of relationship is strong enough between the dependent γ Variable, and multiple χ Variables, suggesting evidence for the Null Hypothesis that Wage Discrimination may exist.

/...................../

Look at it in terms of the type of research method.

Validity

1. The degree to which a test measures what it was designed to measure.
2. The second involves research design. Here the term refers to the degree to which a study supports the intended conclusion drawn from the results.

The validity reflect the fact that RELIABILITY involves freedom from random error and random errors do not correlate with one another. Under these definitions, a test cannot have high validity unless it also has high reliability. However, the concept of validity has expanded substantially beyond this early definition and the classical relationship between REALIBILITY and VALIDITY need not hold for alternative conceptions of RELIABILITY and VALIDITY.

Test validity can be assessed in a number of ways and thorough test VALIDATION typically involves more than one line of evidence in validity of an assessment method (e.g. structured interviews, personality survey, etc) The current standards for educational and psychological measurement.

Reliability

RELIABILITY engineering is the discipline of ensuring that a *system (or a device in general) will perform its intended function(s) when operated in a specified manner for a specified length of time.

[mine; i.e. interview people in the morning on Monday and in the afternoon on Tuesday and will you get the same results from the morning on the Monday].

RELIABILITY engineering is performed throughout the entire life cycle of a system, including development, test, production and operation.

RELIABILITY may be defined in several ways:

3. The idea that something is fit for purpose with respect to time;

4. The capacity of a device or system to perform as designed;

5. The resistance to failure of a device or system;

6. The ability of a device or system to perform a required function under stated conditions for a specified period of <u>time</u>.

7. The probability that a *<u>functional unit</u> will perform its required function for a specified interval under stated conditions. Reliability engineers rely heavily on *<u>statistics.</u>

Comprehensiveness

The principle of COMPREHENSIVE addresses the full range of circumstances, opportunities, and needs of community residents. A COMPREHENSIVE development approach involves constant consideration of the connections among issues, including social services; education and training; economic development; housing and physical revitalisation; and other quality-of-life activities. The charge to think comprehensively calls for working across these various sectors and recognising and reinforcing **positive** connections among them. The readings in this section explore the rationale and the complexities associated with a comprehensive strategy for neighbourhood change.

Coherence

New ideas cannot just be assimilated as such: they must make sense with respect to what the subject already knows. Existing beliefs provide a "scaffolding" needed to support new ideas. This requirement for ideas to "fit in" the pre-existing cognitive system may be called COHERENCE.

The problem remains to define what "coherence" precisely means mere consisting is clearly not sufficient since any collection of unrelated facts logically consistent in addition, coherence requires connection and mutual support of the different beliefs.

Since learning is based on the strengthening of associations, idea that do not connect to existing knowledge simply cannot be learnt.

Connection means some kind of a <u>semantic</u> or associative relationship so that information about one idea also gives you some information about the other. An idea can furthermore support another idea by providing an explanation, evidence or arguments why the latter idea should be true. The preference for CONSISTENCY can be motivated by the theory of cognitive dissonance, which states that <u>people tend to reject idea s that</u> <u>contradict what they already believe.</u>

More generally, it follows from the fact that a fits, individual must be able to make clear-cut decisions. Mutually contradictory rules will create a situation of confusion or hesitation, which is likely to diminish the chances for survival, coherence as a criterion of truth [the coherence theory of truth first published Tue sep

3, 1996; substantive revision Thu may 31, 2001 – A coherence theory of truth, states that the truth of any (true) proposition consists in its coherence with some specified set or propositions. The coherence theory differs from its principle competitor, the correspondence theory of truth, in two essential respects] is emphasised by EPISTEMOLOGY of constructivism [follows 2 principles (1) knowledge is not passively received either through the senses or by way or communication, but is actually built up by cognising subject. (2) The function of cognition is adaptive and serves the subject's organisation of the experiential world, not the discovery of an objective ONTOLOGICAL

- Validity (the degree to which the research study results supports the intended conclusion.
- Reliability (the idea that under specific conditions, the research study results fits the time and purpose for which it was designed
- .Comprehensiveness (the research study results shows connections among issues e.g.social services, education and training, economic development and housing
- Coherence (the requirement for the research study results to 'fit' pre-exisiting believes

/…..……………/

CHAPTER 1

LAW

What is law?

'Law ... is definable as a system of rules. It guides and directs our activities in much of day to day life: the purchases we make in a shop, our conduct at work and our relationship with the state are all built upon the foundation of legal rules' (Holland and Webb, 1996).

Why do we need law?

Almost everything we do is governed by some set rules. For example, there are rules set by Games for social clubs, for sports and rules set by employers for adults employees in the workplace.

There are also rules imposed by morality (regulating abnormal behaviours, behaviours that pose a threat to the normal behaviours fabric of society / elite) and custom e.g. British Custom of Government legislation called 'Acts' of Parliament e.g. Employment Act 1998, Crime Act 1998 (Home Office) and court case law decided by House of Lords (the two main sources of law in this country UK) that play an important role in telling us what we should and should not do.

Further clarification about the scope, purpose and interpretation of an Act is provided by Case Law. Cases which are decided by the House of Lords, the most senior court in England, are binding on all lower courts. Cases decided by the Court of Appeal are binding on lower courts.

A further source of law derives from the European Convention on Human Rights (ECHR) and Fundamental Freedoms

However, some rules -- those made by the state (in the form of government legislation) called 'ACTS' of Parliament e.g. Employment Act 1998, Crime Act 1998 (Home Office) or the courts (in the form of case law) case law decided by House of Lords are called laws and are the two main sources of law (courts and state)

Further clarification about the scope, purpose and interpretation of an Act is provided by Case Law. Cases which are decided by the House of Lords, the most senior court in England, are binding on all lower courts. Cases decided by the Court of Appeal are binding on lower courts.

A further source of law derives from the European Convention on Human Rights (ECHR) and Fundamental Freedoms, which is overseen by the European Court of Human Rights.

Prior to October 2000 this Convention was not integrated into English law and, therefore, any person who believed that their human rights had been abused had to pursue their case through the English courts and if dissatisfied with the outcome, petition the European Court of Human Rights for a hearing.

Laws resemble morality because they are designed to control or alter behaviour (how one should behave)

Unlike rules of morality, laws are enforced if one breach or breaks a law -- whether they like it or not -- they may be forced to pay a fine, pay damages or go to prison.

see case Entick v (against) Carrington (1765), also note A.V. Dicey in constitutional law. Dicey's Rule of Law, no-one is above the law except for the administrator of the state given special powers to enforce the rule of law / the law..

For information, rule of law - is disputes between government and the citizen settled in ordinary courts.

'GOALS OF THE LAW'

In the United Kingdom, laws are not only designed to be govern our conduct (behaviour) they also intended to give effect to social policies (advocacy on social action pertaining to given voice and action to rights of a group of citizens / people affected by error in law).

Social policy, For example, some laws provide for benefits when workers are injured on the job - (rights / workers rights/ employment rights) (made law through social campaign action of social policy action). Also, for health care, as well as for student loans to students who otherwise might not be able to go to university.

****

ANOTHER GOAL IS **FAIRNESS**

****

Fairness means that the law should recognise and protect certain basic individual rights and freedoms such as liberty and equality. (see equality before the law , a.v. dicey , pepper v hart (1993), armory v delamirie a boy chimney finds a jewel / ring , boy takes it to a shop to be valued, after valuation, boy decides to keep the jewel, shop goldsmith apprentice hands back the jewel but had removed the stone in the jewel, Court saw it as Finders Keepers in favour of the boy chimney sweep.

(see the Leviathan - life is wicked brutish and short without laws protecting the liberty of e.g. another man's property , the individual and the state).

The law also serves to ensure that strong groups and individuals do not use their powerful positions to take unfair advantage of weaker individuals.

However despite these best intentions, laws are sometimes created that people later recognise as being of unjust, unfair practice. (here judicial review, judge remedies a correction of the error in the law that is causing problems for a group or society, also literal rule and golden rule).

In a democratic society, like Canada, laws are not carved in stone (often resembling the rigidity of a codified / written constitution). However, but most laws reflect the changing needs of society (e.g. flexibility of unwritten constitution). Britain has an unwritten constitution.

In a democracy (elected government accountable to the electorate / voters, power to vote and have a say in who is in power and decisions affecting society. However, and anyone who feels that a particular law is flawed has the right to speak out publicly and to see to change by lawful means (e.g. advocating through social policy through campaigning and social action).

A TORT means 'WRONG'. Law of TORT is about getting fairness, justice remedy out of a wrongful act remedied through compensation, personal injury claims, insurance claim, by compensating a payout for the loss of the individual , claimant they have suffered as a result of the accident.

CHAPTER 2

MATHS

SIMULATANEOUS EQUATIONS
Two types of methods exist: ELIMINATION and SUBSTITUTION

Using the ELIMINATION Method: When to use SUBTRACT or ADDITION.

📁✍ If the **y** in equation (A) has a <u>positive sign</u> and the **y** in equation (B) has <u>a positive sign</u>, SUBTRACT one equation from the other to get rid of the **y** in both equation (A) and equation (B).

To **eliminate** both y's, first check that the value of **y** in equation (A) and equation (B) are the same (i.e. they are both 2y for example). If they are not the same value, make the value of **y** in equation (A) the same as the value of **y** in equation (B) by multiplying.

Example: Equation (A) $x + 4y = 11$
                 Equation (B) $2x + y = 1$ (Both signs are positive)

To give   (A) $x + 4y = 11$
                4 x (B) $8x + 4y = 4$

SUBTRACT equation (A) from equation (B)

To give: $4(B) - (A) \Rightarrow 4y - 4y = 0$ (eliminate y from both equations)

            $4(B) - (A) \Rightarrow 8x - x = 4 - 11$

            $\Rightarrow 7x = -7$

            $\Rightarrow x = \dfrac{-7}{7}$ (take 7 over to the other side)

            $\Rightarrow x = -1$

Now, put into one equation the value of x to find the value of **y**:
        Using equation (A) $-1 + 4y = 11$
                $\Rightarrow \quad 4y = 11 + 1$
                $\Rightarrow \quad 4y = 12$
                $y = \dfrac{12}{4}$

                $y = 3$

Finally check values satisfy by substituting the value of χ and y in to equation (A) and (B).

Equation (A) -1 + 4 x 3 = 11
Equation (B) 2 x -1 + 3 = 1

Using the ELIMINATION Method: When to use SUBTRACT or ADDITION.

📖☞ When the value of **y** in one equation is <u>negative</u> and the value of **y** in the other equation is <u>positive</u>, ADD both equations together.

To **eliminate** both y's, first check that the value of **y** in equation (A) and equation (B) are the same (i.e. they are both 2y for example). If they are not the same value, make the value of **y** in equation (A) the same as the value of **y** in equation (B) by multiplying.

Example: Equation (A) $2\chi +$ y = 40

Equation (B) $3\chi - 2y = 4$ (One sign is positive, the other is negative)

To give   2 x (A) $4\chi + 2y = 80$
            (B) $3\chi - 2y = 4$

ADD equation (A) and equation (B)

To give   2(A) + (B) $\Rightarrow$ $2y + (- 2y) = 0$ (eliminate y from both equations)

            2(A) + (B) $\Rightarrow$ $4\chi + 3\chi = 80 + 4$

            $\Rightarrow$ $7\chi = 84$

            $\Rightarrow$ $\chi = \dfrac{84}{7}$ (take 7 over to the other side)

$$\chi = 12$$

Now, put into one equation the value of χ to find the value of y:

Using equation (A) $2 \times 12 + y = 40$

$$\Rightarrow \quad y = 40 - 24$$
$$\Rightarrow \quad y = 16$$

Finally check values satisfy by substituting the value of χ and y in to equation (A) and (B).

Equation (A) $2 \times 12 + 16 = 40$

Equation (B) $3 \times 12 - 2 \times 16 = 4$

Using the SUBSTITUTION Method

📃☞ Rearrange one equation to read either

- "y = ..." or

- "χ = ..."

Example: Equation (A) $\chi + 4y = 11$
              Equation (B) $2\chi + y = 1$

Rearrange Equation (B) to read ' y= ' $\rightarrow y = 1 - 2\chi$

Substitute Equation (B) into Equation (A)

$$\chi + 4(1 - 2\chi) = 11 \qquad \text{[Simplify } 4(1 - 2\chi) \text{]}$$

$$\chi + 4 - 8\chi = 11$$

$$-7\chi = 11 - 4$$

$$\chi = \frac{7}{-7} \qquad \text{(take - 7 to the other side)}$$

$$\chi = -1$$

Now put (substitute) value of χ back into Equation (B) to find the value of y:

Equation (B) $\quad$ *2 x –1 + y = 1*

-2 + y = 1

Y = 3

CHAPTER 2

MATHS

<u>Investigation: Rate of Reaction</u>
<u>Brief</u>
In this investigation I am going to find out if changing the size of the pieces of calcium carbonate ($CaCO_3$), affects the time taken for the marble (calcium carbonate, $CaCO_3$) to completely dissolve. I will be testing four different sizes of calcium carbonate pieces.

<u>Aim</u>
I will be investigating the effect marble chips (calcium carbonate, $CaCO_3$) surface area has on the rate of reaction when diluted with hydrochloric acid. By surface area I mean the size of the calcium carbonate pieces which will be tested in:
• powdered form
• small form
• medium form
• large form

Although the surface area of the calcium carbonate will change in each case of the experiment, the mass (in grams) of the marble however, will be kept the same throughout, for fair testing.

The amount of hydrochloric acid used (in ml) will also be kept the same to keep the investigation a fair one. This is because, for example, if the amount of calcium carbonate (in grams) used is increased while the hydrochloric acid is kept the same then this can cause the rate of reaction to be slower.

Also, the remaining variables below will be kept the same for the following reasons: -

- Concentration of hydrochloric acid: (an increase in the concentration of hydrochloric acid could speed up the rate of reaction)

Increasing the concentration of the hydrochloric acid will increase the number of particles present. This will increase the chance of the particles colliding and so will speed up the rate of reaction.

- Temperature. (an increase in the temperature can double the rate of reaction)

Increasing the temperature of the reactants provides the particles with more <u>kinetic energy</u>, so they will move faster. This increases the number of collisions per second, and hence increases the rate of reaction. For example, increasing the temperature of the Hydrochloric acid will increase the speed of the Hydrochloric acid particles so that the number of collisions per second is increased.

Equipment/Resources

1. Cotton wool (x 1) to trap acid particles that may spray out during the reaction process.
2. Conical flask (x 1) to dilute hydrochloric acid and marble chips.
3. 50g Calcium Carbonate or Marble chips ($CaCO_3$) (x 4: powdered, small, medium and large)
4. 50ml Hydrochloric Acid (HCl) (x 4)
5. Scale (to measure the amount of calcium carbonate needed)
6. Stop watch (to record the time taken for the marble to dissolve in the hydrochloric acid)

Method

For this experiment, I will set out the equipment/resources stated above.

Next, I will pour 50g of calcium carbonate into a conical flask, followed by 50ml of hydrochloric acid. I will then measure the rate of reaction using a stop watch and record my findings on a table. The experiment will be repeated four times using different size marble chips each time (powdered, small, medium and large). I will also attempt the experiment twice and I will take an average reading of the results.

Safety hazards for hydrochloric acid and calcium carbonate and general lab safety.
*Wear goggles
*Wear gloves when handling hydrochloric acid
*Use cotton wool over the conical flask that I will be using to carry out my experiment to stop any sprays of hydrochloric acid during reaction process.
*Keep the laboratory floor clear of any objects that is likely to make me trip or fall

Prediction / Hypothesis

I predict that the larger the surface area of the calcium carbonate pieces, the more contact it has with the hydrochloric acid particles and thus the more collisions per second taking place and so the calcium carbonate pieces is likely to completely dissolve more quickly. For example I predict that the powdered calcium carbonate pieces of which has the largest surface area will dissolve more quickly in the hydrochloric acid solution that the small, medium and large calcium carbonate pieces.

Diagram

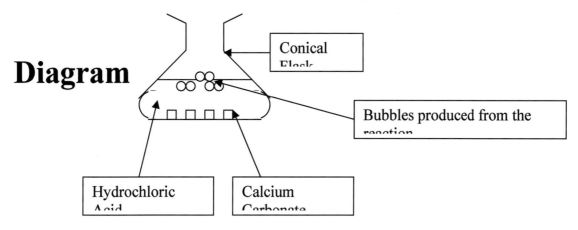

Table of Results

Surface area of Calcium Carbonate	Volume of Hydrochloric Acid (ml)	Time taken to react (secs)		
		First attempt	Second attempt	→ Average time taken to react (secs)
Powered (50g)	50	19	118	19 + 118 / 2 = 78
Small chips (50g)	50	744	576	744 + 576 / 2 = 1032
Medium chips (50g)	50	1228	1235	1228 + 1235 / 2 = 1845.5
Large chips (50g)	50	1531	1451	1531 + 1451 / 2 = 2256.5

The table of results shows what I found out from diluting 50g of powdered, small, medium and large calcium carbonate pieces in 50ml of hydrochloric acid. I found out that the larger the surface area of the calcium carbonate pieces, the quicker the rate of reaction (the quicker the time taken for the calcium carbonate pieces to dissolve in the hydrochloric acid particles). The table also shows the average time taken for the calcium carbonate pieces to dissolve in the hydrochloric acid solution in each of the four cases using powdered, small medium and large calcium carbonate pieces.

Graph:

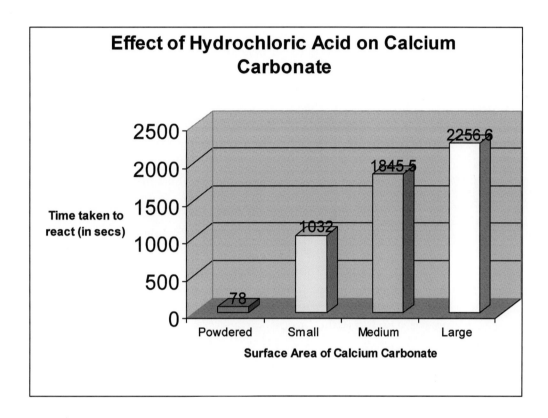

Evaluation

My experiment went well and was a fair and reliable one. I followed the safety rules and used the correct measurement of hydrochloric acid (of 50ml) and calcium carbonate (of 50g) each time to get a fair reading. I also changed the surface area of the calcium carbonate each time in order to test the effect the rate of reaction the 50ml of hydrochloric acid had on the surface area of the marble chips. However, I did encounter a mild difficulty with using the electronic scale to measure the 50g of calcium carbonate. This is because the scale is sensitive and would give a reading less or more than 50g and I would have to reduce or add more calcium carbonate to get the reading on the scale to read 50g precisely. I also noticed a huge time difference between the first attempt and second attempt to test the rate of reaction the hydrochloric acid had on the surface area of the powdered calcium carbonate pieces. The reading of the first attempt is 19 seconds while the reading of the second attempt is 118. I think the huge difference between the first attempt reading and the second attempt reading might be partly due to a cooler room temperature (in the case of the second attempt reading) and the settling of the hydrochloric acid particles after transporting the hydrochloric acid from its storage place to the lab table, since it was the first experiment.

From the experiment, I found out that changing the size of the pieces of calcium carbonate affects the rate of reaction - the time taken for the calcium carbonate pieces to completely dissolve in the hydrochloric acid. I also found out that the larger the surface area of the calcium carbonate pieces, the more contact the calcium carbonate pieces comes in contact with the hydrochloric acid particles and so there is more kinetic energy which speeds up the rate of reaction. For example the first attempt to record the rate of reaction – the time taken in seconds for the 50g of powdered calcium carbonate pieces to completely dissolve in the 50ml of hydrochloric acid was recorded at 19 secs while the time taken in seconds for the 50g of large calcium carbonate pieces to completely dissolve in the 50ml of hydrochloric acid took 1531 secs.

Also, I predicted that the greater the surface area of the calcium carbonate pieces, the contact it has with the hydrochloric acid particles and thus the more collisions per second taken place and so the calcium carbonate pieces is likely to dissolve more quickly in the hydrochloric acid solution. My table of results shows that my prediction is correct. For example the average time taken for the 50g of powdered calcium carbonate pieces (of which has the largest surface area) taken to dissolve in the 50ml of hydrochloric acid particles is 78 seconds while the average time taken for the 50g of large calcium carbonate pieces (of which has the smallest surface area) taken to dissolve in the 50ml of hydrochloric acid particles is 2256.5.

Alongside, I think the experiment could be improved by ensuring the room temperature is kept the same throughout and also ensuring that when the hydrochloric acid is transported from its storage place, sufficient time is left for the particles to settle. This is so that the first and second attempt reading and not far apart as in the case of the powdered calcium carbonate pieces. The first attempt reading is 19 seconds and the second attempt reading is 1531 seconds.

Nonetheless, I think this is a good experiment to carry out because it shows how the surface are of the marble chips (calcium carbonate pieces) can have an effect on the rate of reaction.

Bibliography:

Encarta CD-Rom
Letts GCSE Revision Guide
Classwork notes: rocks

CHAPTER 2

MATHS

Question 1 (Numerical Relationships)

(i) A psychologist asked 12 people to complete a task. The time taken (in minutes) for each person to complete the task is shown in Table 1.

Table 1: Time to Complete Task (minutes)											
32	33	39	25	29	29	30	34	26	21	28	31

Mean is Adding up all values and dividing by the number of values there are:

$$\frac{32+33+39+25+29+29+30+34+26+21+28+31}{12} = \frac{357}{12} = 29.75$$

Thus the Mean time taken to complete the task is 29.75 minutes

(ii) An Open University student gains the scores shown in Table 2 on assignments during a course.

Table 2: A Student's scores		
Number	**Score**	**Weight**
01	55	10
02	60	15
03	54	15
04	72	20
05	69	40

Calculate the student's weighted mean score.

number	Score	Weight		
			$85 \times 10 = 850$	Or $85 \times 0.1 = 8.5$
			$60 \times 15 = 900$	Or $60 \times 0.15 = 9$
			$54 \times 15 = 810$	Or $54 \times 0.15 = 8.1$
			$72 \times 20 = 1440$	Or $72 \times 0.2 = 14.4$
			$69 \times 40 = 2760$	Or $69 \times 0.4 = 27.6$
			Total = 6760	Total = 67.6

Σ (sum of) , totalling the equation of

X (MEAN)

W (weight)

Σ (sum of)
χ (MEAN) and
w (weight)

$$\text{Weighted Mean} = \frac{\Sigma \chi w}{\Sigma w} = \frac{6760}{100} = 67.6$$

Thus the student's weighted mean score is 67.6

(iii) Table 3 shoes the average price of a dozen size 2 eggs at selected dates during 2006.

Table 3: The average price of a dozen size 2 eggs in 2006 (Source: Office for National Statistics)			
Month	February	June	October
Price (£)	1.75	1.79	1.87

(a) Find the percentage rise in the average price of a dozen size 2 eggs between February and June, giving your answer correct to 1 decimal place.

$\rightarrow$ Percentage Increase or Rise $\dfrac{\text{Change}}{\text{Original}} \times 100$

$\rightarrow$

$$\frac{1.79 - 1.75}{1.75} = \frac{0.04}{1.75} = 0.0228571 \rightarrow 0.0228571 \times 100 = 2.28571\% \rightarrow 2.2\%\_to\_1\_decimal\_place$$

Thus, the percentage rise in the average price of a dozen size 2 eggs between February and June is 2.2%.

(b) Using the methods in Section 3 of Unit2, construct a price index for the average price of size 2 eggs. Use February 2006 as the base month with a price index of 100, and calcuate the price indices for June and October. Give your answers correct to 1 decimal place.

Price Indices (Price Index)

Month	February 2006	June 2006	October 2006
Price (£)	1.75	1.79	1.87
Price Ratio	1.000 (base month)	$\dfrac{1.79}{1.75} = 1.022857143$	$\dfrac{1.87}{1.75} = 1.068571429$
Price Index	$1.000 \times 100 = 100$	1.022857143×100 = **102.3 to 1 decimal place**	1.068571429×100 = **106.9 to 1 decimal place**

137

(iv) In this part fo the question, you are asked to demonstrate your understanding of your work on *finding and using averagtes of data sets.*

(a) Choose an example of your work from which uses atype of average different from those in parts (1) and (ii) of the question. Your example can be a or question or an activity or exercise form the course, which demonstrates your understanding of using an average.

Include your original working for your example, or a photocopy, giving a full reference (e.g. assignment number and question number or unit number, page number and acitivity number).

Your tutor will be looking for evidence that you understood this topic, so annotate your working to show this by

> ➤ Marking the secton of your work that is relevant;
> ➤ Explaining why an average was used in your example.

Table 4 shows the times (in minutes) taken by eight runners to complete a marathon

Table 4 Times taken to complete a marathon (minutes)							
188	209	173	222	256	195	184	230

Answer to Question 6: The option that gives the Median (in minutes) of these times is 202 (minutes)

Where the Median is obtained by arranging the values in ascending order and selecting the middle value if the values give an odd number or if the values given and even number then selecting the two middle values and dividing by two (the mean of the two middle values if there the values give an even number and produce two middle values). Thus the Median is:

$$172 \rightarrow 184 \rightarrow 188 \rightarrow 195 \rightarrow 209 \rightarrow 222 \rightarrow 230 \rightarrow 256 \rightarrow \frac{195+209}{2} = \frac{404}{2} = 202\_(min\,utes)$$

Answer to Question 7: The option that gives the Mean (in minutes) of these time is 207 (minutes)

Where the Mean is obtained by adding up all the values and dividing by the number of values there are:

$$\frac{172+184+188+195+209+222+230+256}{8} \rightarrow \frac{1656}{8} = 207\_(min\,utes)$$

(b) Referringto your answers in this question and other examples from that use an average:

> ## Describe how two different types of averages may be found

The two different types of averages that I am going to describe are the Mean and the Median.

The Mean can be found by adding up all the values and dividing by the number of values there are - as illustrated in question1 (iv) (a).

The Median can be found by arranging the values in ascending order and selecting the middle value if the values give an odd number or if the values given and even number then selecting the two middle values and dividing by two (the mean of the two middle values if there the values give an even number and produce two middle values) - as illustrated in question1 (iv) (a).

> ## Explain the strengths and weaknesses of the median and the mean.

The Strength of the Mean is that because it proportions the values, it can be a very good average if there are no outliers (very high or very low values that can distort the average) and the values are fairly close to one and other. For example if the values are 1+2+3 = 6, dividing 6 by 3 (number of values there are) gives a Mean average of 3 which is close to the middle value of 2 as there are no outliers that can distort the value of the Mean.

However if there are outliers, this could distort the authenticity of the Mean. For example if the values are 1+2+21 = 24, dividing 24 by 3 (the number of values there are) gives a Mean average of 8 which is not close to the middle value of 2 as 21 is an abnormally high value which is distorting the value of Mean..

Similarly the Median is a reliable average if there are no outliers (as described above). For example if the values are $1 \rightarrow 2 \rightarrow 3$ gives a middle value of 2 which is close to the other values and thus there are no outliers that can distort the value of Median.

However, if the values are $1 \rightarrow 2 \rightarrow 21$, the Median would be 2 which is not a reliable because it is closer to one of the values and very far apart from the other value, suggesting that there is an outlier which is 21 that is distorting the value of the Median.

Question 2 (Graphs and Diagrams)

The aim of this question is for you to demonstrate your understanding of the use of graphs.

(i) A delivery driver has a choice of routes between two towns. She wants to know which route generally takes less time, so she records the journey times on the two routes over a number of weeks. Her results are shown in Table 4.

Table 4: Journey times between two towns	
Journey time for route A (minutes)	**Journey time for route B (minutes)**
63	59
59	64
62	70
60	58
58	56
57	61
65	68
61	60
54	60
60	55
64	65
58	68
	65
	61

(a) Using a common axis, draw accurate box plots to illustrate these data.

Please refer to separate sheet attached

(b) Use your boxplots to compare the journey times for the two routes

Looking at the Box Plots for Route A and Route B: the Median Average Journey time for Route A is 60 minutes, Similarly the Median Average Journey for Route B is 60.5 minutes close to 60 minutes.

Besides, the fact that both the Median Average Journey Time for Route A and Route B are fairly similar, there is no guarantee that Route B will be quicker journey Route and take less time than Route A. This is because Route B has a **left skewed average Median,** e.g. the average Median of the Box plot for Route B is not in the middle of the box plot, it is off-centre and leaning towards the left of the box plot. This left tendency suggest that the average Median for Route B is Biased. Alongside, the box plot for **Route B has an outlier**. This outlier gives an abnormally high time taken for one of the times recorded for the Delivery Driver if she took Route B. For this reason Route B is not a good record when taking into consideration 'go slow' or heavy traffic which can increase the time taken to travel the route.

Whereas, with the Box Plot for Route A, the Mean Average has a slight central tendency as the Box plot for Route is slightly evenly proportioned as the Box Plot for Route A is a Median Average value is close to the highest and lowest values. This closeness between the values suggest that Route A is a good record when taking into consideration 'go slow' or heavy traffic and will always guarantee less time taken than Route B.

(ii) (a) Find the equation of the straight line that passes through the points (-1, -5) and (2, 4)

Linear equation (straight line) is $y = m\chi + c$

Where m = Gradient and c = y intercept or constant

$(\chi, y) \rightarrow$(-1, -5) and (2, 4)

Gradient (m) $\rightarrow \dfrac{y2 - y1}{x2 - x1} = \dfrac{4 - -5}{2 - -5} = \dfrac{9}{7} = 1.285714286$

$\therefore$ Gradient (m) $= 1.285714286$

$\therefore y = 1.285714286 \times \chi + c$

Substitute **(-1, -5)** into $y = m\chi + c$

Where $\chi = -1$ and $y = -5$

$-5 = (1.285714286 \times -1) + c$

$-5 = -1.285714286 \times -1 + c$

$-5 + 1.285714286 = c$

$-3.714285714 = c$ or $c = -3.714285714$

Proof:
Thus equation is $y \rightarrow 1.285714286 \times -1 + -3.714285714 = -5$

Or $y \rightarrow 1.3 \times -1 + 3.7 = -5$

Or $y = m\chi + c$

Rearrange to make χ the subject:

$Y - c = m\chi \rightarrow \dfrac{y-c}{m} = x \rightarrow \dfrac{-5+3.7}{1.3} = -1.3$

$\chi = -1$

(ii)(b) Find the points where the line $2x + 5y = 10$ crosses the x-axis and the y-axis

For x:
$2x + 5y = 10$

$2x + 5(0) = 10$, where $5 \times 0 = 0$, gives

$2x = 10$

$\dfrac{2x}{2} = \dfrac{10}{2} = 5$

$x = 5$

x intercept $\rightarrow$ (5,0), where $x = 5$ and $y = 0$

For y:
$2x + 5y = 10$

$2(0) + 5y = 10$, where $2 \times 0 = 0$, gives

$5y = 10$

$\dfrac{5y}{5} = \dfrac{10}{5} = 2$

$y = 2$

y intercept $\rightarrow$ (0,2), where $x = 0$ and $y = 2$

Proof:

$2x + 5y = 10$

$2(5) + 5(2) = 10$

$2x = 10 - 5y$

$2(5) = 10 - 5(2)$

$10 = 10 - 10$

$10 = 0$

Or

$5y = 10 - 2\chi$

$5(2) = 10 - 2(5)$

$10 = 10 - 10$

$10 = 0$

(c) Find the vertex of the parobola $y = \chi^2 + 4\chi + 1$

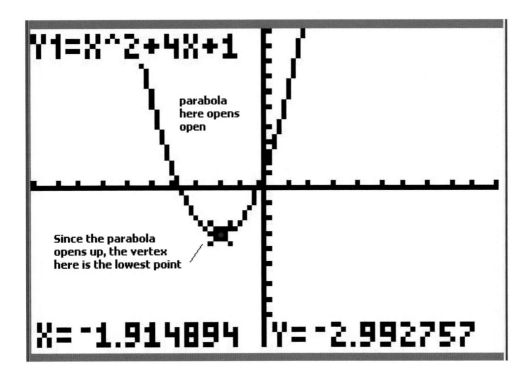

Thus vertex is at: x = -1.914894 and y = -2.992757

Question 2 (iii) In this part of the question, you are asked to demonstrate your understanding of your work form on using graphs to help *answer questions in a practical concext.*

(a) Choose an example of your work from where you have used a graph, *other than a boxplot,* to help answer a question in a practical contex. You example can be a or question or an activity or exercise from the course, which demonstrates your understanding of using a graph to help answer a question in a practical context.

Include your original working for your example, or a photocopy, giving a full reference (e.e. assigment number and question number or unit number, page number and activity number).

Your tutor will be looking for evidence that you understand this topic, so annotate your work to show this by:

  ➢ Marking the section of your work that is relevant;

  ➢ Stating both the question that you asked, and the answer that you found.

(b) Referring to your answers in this question and other examples from , describe <u>two different types of graph</u> that can be used to help answer a question in a practical context. Your description should include:

  ➢ The kind of information or data that you need for the graph;
  ➢ How the graph is constructed;
  ➢ How the graph can be used to answer a question.

As a guide, you answer should be tween 150 and 300 words.

, 03, Question 2 Assignment Booklet page 41

Question 2

The tariffs for two electricity suppliers are given in the table below.

Tariffs for two electricity suppliers

	Standing charge per month/pounds	Price per unit/pounds
Supplier 1	10	0.14
Supplier 2	14	0.11

(i) the table below shows how the total monthly charges under the two suppliers compare for differing amounts of electricity consumption per month.

Charges under two electricity suppliers

Units used per month	0	100	200	500
Suplier 1/ pounds	10	24	38	80
Suplier 2 / pounds	14	25	36	69

(iii) On squared paper, draw graphs of the two functions from part (ii), on the same axes, with cost on the vertical axis and adding appropriate labelling

Please refer to separate sheet attached

(iv) The lines representing these functions intersect. Write down the approximate coordinates of the intersection point. What does this point represent?

(133, 27), where x = 133 and y = 27

(b) Referring to your answers in this question and other examples from , describe <u>two different types of graph</u> that can be used to help answer a question in a practical context. Your description should include:

- ➤ **The kind of information or data that you need for the graph;**
- ➤ **How the graph is constructed;**
- ➤ **How the graph can be used to answer a question.**

Two types of graphs than can be used to hep answer a question is straight line graph as describe above and a scatter plot as used in   02 Question 1 (ii) (a).

A **straight line graph** is constructed using a horizontal x and vertical y axis.

A **straight line graph** is an appropriate way of interpreting information (data) as it gives a visual picture of the information (data). The straight line graph can be used to answer a question as it can indicate a trend. This trend can be used to make a prediction such as when x = 133 and y = 27, (as described above in my example of graphs) both suppliers charge the same amount on electricity.

Using x and y coordinates, a **scatterplot** is constructed for a data one wants to anaylse. The data is analysed by plotting the data on a scatterplot/scattergraph of dots.

A **scatterplot** is an appropriate way to display two types of data because it shows (usefully) the relationships (if any exists) of two variables: *x* and *y* group of i.e. annual number of primary teachig hours and the average mathematical scores when answering a question. In other words, it appropriately shows the relationshiup between the annual number of primary teaching hours and the average mathematical scores

Question 3 (Functions and symbols)

The aim of this question is to for you to demonstrate your understanding of using formulas and solving equations

(i) Solve the following equations. In each case, show your methods clearly.

(a) $5\chi - 1 = 9$
(b) $6 + \chi = 5 - 2(\chi + 1)$
(c) $\chi^2 + 2x = 0$

(a) $5\chi - 1 = 9$

$5\chi - 1 = 9$

$5\chi = 9 + 1$

$5\chi = 10$

$$\frac{5x}{5} = \frac{10}{5}$$

$\chi = 2$

Proof
$5\chi - 1 = 9$

$5(2) - 1 = 9$

$10 - 1 = 9$

(b) $6 + \chi = 5 - 2(\chi + 1)$

$6 + \chi = 5 - 2(\chi + 1)$

$6 + \chi = 3(\chi + 1)$

$6 + \chi = 3(\chi) + 3(1)$

$6 + \chi = 3\chi + 3$

$6 - 3 = 3\chi - \chi$

$3 = 2\chi$

$\dfrac{3}{2} = \dfrac{2x}{2} = 1.5, \rightarrow x = 1.5$

$\chi = 1.5$

Proof:
$6 + \chi = 5 - 2(\chi + 1)$

$6 + 1.5 = 3(1.5 + 1)$

$7.5 = 3(1.5) + 3(1)$

$7.5 = 4.5 + 3$

$7.5 = 7.5$

(c) $\chi^2 + 2x = 0$

$\chi(\chi + 2) = 0$

$\chi = 0$ and $\chi = -2$

(ii) Use your course calculator to find the solution that lies between 0 and 1 of the equation

$$1 - \frac{5x}{x^2 + 1} = 0,$$

Correct to 3 decimal places

Graph Calculator:

χ intercept $\rightarrow \chi = 0.21276596$ (0.21 to 3 decimal places), and $y = 0$

y intercept $\rightarrow \chi = 0$, and $y = 0.96774194$ (0.97 to 3 decimal places)

(iii) A formula which can be used to find the average length of time T (in hours) which customers spending queuing and being served in a bank with one server is

$$T = \frac{1}{s - a}$$

Where 'a' is the average rate per hour at which customers arrive and join the queue, and 's' is the average rate per hour at which customers are served. (This assumes that 'a' is smaller than 's').

(a) How long on average will a customer spend in the bank if customers arrive a a rate of 20 per hour and are served a rate of 30 per hour on average? Give you answer in minutes.

$$T = \frac{1}{s - a}$$

$$T = \frac{1}{30 - 20} = \frac{1}{10} = 0.1 \_ hours$$

0.1 hours $\times$ 60 minutes = 6 minutes.

Thus on average a customer will spend 6 minutes in the bankj if the customers arrive at a rate of 20 per hour and are served at a rate fo 30 per hour.

(b) Rearrange the formula to make 's' the subject.

$$T = \frac{1}{s-a}, \rightarrow \frac{1}{T} = s - a, \rightarrow \frac{1}{T} + a = s$$

(c) The bank does not wish customers to spend more than 4 minutes, on average, in the bank. Use your formula from part (iii)(b) to find the minimum service rate that would allow this to happen, assuming that the customers continue to arrive at a rate of 20 per hour.

T = 4 minutes and a = 20 per hour arriving customers

$$\frac{4\_\min utes}{60\_\min utes} = 0.066666666\_hours, \text{ Thus T} = 0.066666666 \text{ hours}$$

$$s = \frac{1}{T} + a, \rightarrow \frac{1}{0.066666666} + 20, \rightarrow 15.0000001 + 20 = 35.00000015 \therefore s = 35\_\min utes$$

(iv) In this part of the question, you are asked to demonstrate your understanding of your work from on *solving equations*.

(a) Choose an example of your work from where one or more equations have been solved in a practical context. Your example can be a or question or an activity or exercise from the course, which demonstrates your understanding of solving equations in a practical context.

Include your original working for your example, or a photocopy, giving a full reference (e.e. assignment number and question number or unit number, page number and activity number).

Your tutor will be looking for evidence that you understand this topic, so annotate you work to show this by:

➢ Marking the section of your work that is relevant;
➢ Explaining how the solution of the equation is interpreted in the practical context.

(b) Referrign to your answers in this question and other examples from of solving equations:

➢ Explain what solving an equation means;
➢ Describe two different methods of solving equations

As a guide, your answer should be between 150 and 300 words.

, 03, Question 2 Assignment Booklet page 41

(v) Use algebra to solve the two simultaneous equations from part (ii) so as to obtain the accurate coordinates of the point of intersection. Show your working clearly.

Supplier 1 $\rightarrow$ $y = 10 + 0.14x$
Supplier 2 $\rightarrow$ $y = 14 + 0.11x.$

$0.14x + 10 = 0.11x + 14$

Collect x on one side (including adjusting signs) to give:

$0.14x - 0.11x = 14 - 10$

$\rightarrow 0.03x = 4$, Divide both sides by 0.03 to get x

$$x = \frac{4}{0.03}$$

x = 133.3333333

x = 133.3, **point of intersection at which both suppliers charge the same amount for electricity**

(b) Referring to your answers in this question and other examples from   of solving equations:

> **Explain what solving an equation means;**
> **Describe two different methods of solving equations**

Equations are mathematical statements with one or more letters in place of numbers, but most importantly they contain an equals sign. Formulas/Forumlae are equations which can contain any number of letters in place of numbers as seen above with an example from 03.

Solving an equation means finding the value of the letter or letters that make the mathematical statement true.

Two different methods of solving equation could be firstly in a 'linear equation' could be re-arranging the equation to make the letter the subject on one side of the equation (equal sign).

A second method of solving and equation could be solving **simulataneous equations** through a number of methods including the Elimination Method. The Elimination method of solving a simultaneous equation is initially to eliminate the one variable to find a solution to the other one, and then to substitue the found variable to complete the solution.

CHAPTER 3

POLICY AND THE SOCIAL SCIENCES AND LITERATURE

eBUSINESS

Key words : Electronic Business systems, modern enterprise design, manage and lead //

- Multimedia Design technologies is used to create E-business products and services ; for example, (page 95 Electronic Business Systems, Modern Enterprise Design Manage and Lead) using java and html design to create business marketing artefact (e.g. website) created using multimedia design technology

- E-business theory is used for market structure/analysis: to find out the best market structure for the E-business product ; using business market structure analysis to identify the best marketing techniques for the marketing artefact (e.g. website) created using multimedia design technology.

In E-Business theory, Market analysis is not confined to consumer input and feedback, it should involve gaining all awareness of all factors such as:

(1) Competitors, (2) Suppliers, (3) Economic, (4) technological, (5) legal among others / etc.

MACRO: AGGREGATE WHOLE CONNECTION OF NETWORKS AND
RELATIONSHIP

(1) Competitors: Competition (Policy Act 1998) requires promoting competition in

the market (e.g. UK Market), because competition benefits consumers in the

short run by lowering prices and offering them a wide range of goods and

services. conclusion: is identifying competitors that will allow you to gain

entry into the market that has the capacity for a wide range of suppliers

offering cheaper goods and services //

(2) SUPPLIERS: Trade policies tend to favour free trade. Free trade means

increasing the amount of compeitition from abroad to the UK market but also

allowing UK firms to export more freely to foreign markets. Small firms are

encouraged through a range of schemes and incentives including lower taxes on

profits for small limited companies. Conclusion: Suppliers are firms who

trade goods and services ; Who are your Suppliers small firms or monopoly

firms

//

SUPPLIER SIZE ; Monopolies are powerful (acquisitions and mergers /

conglomeration e.g. owning the means of producing all their production,

supplier and service companies) like Major utilities industries and

pharmaceutical industries tend to create a barrier to entry for competition

and so Competition Government Policy Act 1998 REGULATION (Privatisation,

Regulation and Deregulation) gives Regulators the power to see that the

Monopoly Supplier is working in 'CORPORATE SOCIAL RESPONSIBILITY':
Plugging

the space between the laws that will allow monopoly suppliers to Give smaller

firms the space to compete in the market.

//

(5) LEGAL : Competition Act 1998 : Competition Government Policy Act 1998

REGULATION (Privatisation, Regulation and Deregulation) gives Regulators the

power to see that the Monopoly Supplier is working in 'CORPORATE SOCIAL

RESPONSIBILITY': Plugging the space between the laws that will allow monopoly

suppliers to GIVE smaller firms the space to compete in the market.

//

(4) TECHNOLOGICAL: e.g.
- Computer: PC Operating System Communication e.g. computers are used to talk

to each other ;
- Competition Policy / Competitors: Software which worked on one 'MS Dos'

machine worked on other 'MS Dos' machines even if they were produced by

different manufacturers or suppliers

INPUT TECHNOLOGY / OUTPUT PRODUCTS : TECHNOLOGY INPUTS : e.g.
cutting down

expenditure by using the most efficient fewer inputs that would increase

Outputting more products// Conclusion: Operating Systems we use today use a

fewer inputs e.g. a desktop display, navigation via a mouse rather than

simply a keyboard (time consuming effort) was good enough to attract high

demand enough for more outputting of products//Sell more products//

MICRO: UNITS: HOUSEHOLD, FIRMS, MARKET //

- Suppliers: Apple Mac, Microsoft

- Economies OF Scale : Apple Mac and Microsoft charged a premium price for the package and initially made large profits by winning a small share of the

market (market entry) // Consumer Policy Act saw that Apple's prices were to

high, and Consumer Input and Feedback, customers valued (competition) the ability
to share software

between different machines using MS Dos, was 'cheaper' for them //

Conclusion: manufacturing computers but in licensing operating system which

would become a universal standard (ISO) / Internet Technology Standards (see page
77, Mousavi), that would give consumers what they

want (CONSUMER PREFERENCE THEORY) e.g. Consumer Input & Feedback,
'customers valued (competition) the

ability to share software between different machines using MS Dos, was

'cheaper' for them'

- Legal: Consumer Welfare Policy : Competition that will give consumers more

choice on a wide range of goods and services at a cheaper price e.g. Consumer Input
and Feedback, customers valued (competition) the ability to share software between

different machines using MS Dos, was 'cheaper' for them'

//

TECHNOLOGICAL / THE MUSIC RETAILLING MARKET:

- COMPETITION POLICY: competition between different retailers will be fierce as
the market for Physical CD or DVD declines. Transforming the Industry are digital
downloads, much of it is illegal downloading by the Apple Ipod has taken a dominant
position in the legal download market. Ease of Use of both the iPod player and the
associated iTunes download website have made it an attractive [cheaper packaging]
alternative to buying physical CDs.

Consumer Policy / Consumer Input & Feedback: Listeners can create their own music
anthologies by downloading individual tracks and organising them to suit their own
needs //
Conclusion: my Music Website will be a suitable Mp3 which can be used by different
communication devices even if it is from a different supplier //

fewer INPUT technology / more OUTPUTS product services: Operating Systems we use today use a

fewer inputs e.g. a desktop display, navigation via a mouse rather than

simply a keyboard (time consuming effort) was good enough to attract high

demand enough for more outputting of products e.g. Music Website//

Economies OF Scale and Size of market :The retail leisure market for recorded music is in crisis. Sales of physical music CDs and DVDs are falling sharply. Ged Doherty, the head of Sony BMG's UK operations, predicted two months ago that CD sales would halve within three years. The industry has already claimed two major casualties this year. Music Zone, a UK chain with 104 stores and 1 100 staff went into administration. HMV is struggling to maintain profitability and find a format which will transform its fortunes.//

Music Specialist like HMV and Music Zone had just under half the market. Supermarkets accounted for around one quarter whilst multiples such as Woolworths had a little over 10 per cent

Transforming the Industries are Digital Downloads

Economies of Scale means: increasing and decreasing returns to scale where the size of the plant of Larger firms increase returns to scale of production of services 'demanded by consumers'. They do this by 'efficiently' using cheaper money saving fewer INPUTS that enables efficient OUTPUT production of goods and services //decreasing returns to scale arise where the size of larger firms do not not have the right cheaper equipment inputs to produce efficient products goods and services to customer 'demand', taste and satisfaction //

Also buying raw materials in bulk enables these firms to secure lower / cheaper prices for their factor 'inputs'

///

PAGE 15 – 17 (Mousavi): Electronic Business Systems Modern Enterprise Design Manage and Lead:

Key Characteristics of the Internet and World-Wide-Web and their influence on B-to-B commerce:

One can list the key features of Internet for commerce as [Timmers 2000];

- AVAILABILITY: Time constraints prevailing in traditional 9-5 businesses do not exist. With online 24 hours 7 days a week immediate Internet access transactions / auctions / exhibitions of products is possible round the clock.

- OMNIPRESENT : Internet access is and will continue to be part of every business facility, just as fax machines, telephones and computers have come.

- GLOBAL ACCESSIBILITY: With no physical boundaries there are no limitations for access from around the world. Business partners and customers can access information of products from the four corners fo the globe.

- Local Accessibility: Internet not only facilities global commerce it also creates a perfect platform to reinforce local presence and person-to-person relationships. Customised websites, e-mail services, SMS for mobile users and user profiles (Cookies) have all contributed to reinforce local presence.

- DIGITALISATION : The business happens in information space even for physical products, Thus improving speed and efficiency in business transactions.

- MULTIMEDIA: A suite of technology have been combined together to offer business a competitive more interactive, and entertaining edge during and selling products [CONSUMER INPUT AND FEEDBACK]

- INTERACTIVITY: It is a challenging task to replace face-to-face business relationship with a virtual one. Internet techology should create an opportunity for improvement in customer service a an affordable price.

- ONE-TO-ONE: Customer profiling and close interactivity enables a strong, one-to-one marketing tool that will enhance business on the Internet.

- NETWORKING EFFECT (GAINING MARKET ENTRY, COMPETITION POLICY): With new businesses joining the WWW the opportunity to connect with others and develop business networks is phenomenal. Various industries can create open markets for virtual communities and third-party marketplaces.

- INTEGRATION: The Internet technology provides the basis for value-chain functions and information integration. Advanced e-Commerce companies are successful in exploiting this technology for added value.

//

CHARACTERISTICS OF B-TO-B MARKETS :

CUSTOMISATION: Products are tailored to consumer requirements

KNOWLEDGE: Knowledge-based interactions with professional customers. The retailer should be well informed about the product

- PERSONAL : Bi-directional relationship with customers, direct interaction between seller and buyer alongside the distribution and resellers

- PROFESSIONAL: Special promotions via brochures, datasheets, videos, tradeshows and exhibitions.

- NEGOTIATIONS: Possibility of negotiations on price, product specifications, delivery time, and payment arrangements.

- MULTI-PARTY: Possiblity of a number of purchaser being involved in the buying process that can be complex and may require extensive procedures.

- MULTI-CHANNELS [ALLOWING ENTRY INTO THE MARKET]: Manufacturers may have different channels to supply different customers e.g. direct sales, agents, distributors, and wholesalers; where there may be conflicting interests amongst business partners.

- INTERNATIONAL [INTERNATIONAL TRADE Trade policies / ALLOWING FOREIGN COMPEITION POLICY]: Globalisation international trade requires its own regulations, different languages, and measures to appreciate diversity of cultures

//

(in text reference: Mousavi, (2008), p158)

Mousavi , page 121 ; 2008 ; p158:

COMPETITION GOVERNNMENT POLICY ACT 1998 can be linked to Mousavi 'E-Commerce: What to do'
that identifying competitors that will allow you to gain

entry into the market that has the capacity for a wide range of suppliers

offering cheaper goods and services: Mousavi 'Ecommerce What to do' supports this that:

- Revolve your companies operations around the customer [CUSTOMER INPUT & FEEDBACK SATISFACTION]

- Avoid falling into the trap of online price wars; DUOPOLY markets which consists of very small number of firms / 2 or 3 firms who dominate the market by creating a BARRIERS TO ENTRY in the market restricting SMALLER FIRMS from gaining entry into the market to compete also // DUOPOLY SHORT TERM PRICE WARS drive down market prices below the market level Supply equals Demand, and forcing them back up again to monopoly high prices making it difficult for smaller firms to gain entry in the market because they do not have the efficient INPUT/OUTPUT to offer these same SHORT TERM LOWER PRICES,only market level Supply=Demand prices //

- BUILD VALUE NETWORKS THAT WILL CONSOLIDATE YOUR RELATIONSHIPS: DMANSAM MUSIC uses ISO / International Standard / Internet Technology Standards (see page 77, Mousavi) that enables music to be STREAMLINED downloaded unto any music Ipod / music player produced by any Supplier//

- YOUR VALUE NETWORK IS LIKE A PROCESS FACTORY THAT SUPPORTS YOUR KEY RELATIONSHIPS : see above

- YOUR EXPERIENCE AND CUSTOMER KNOWLEDGE PROVIDE A RESERVOIR OF COMPETITIVE ADVANTAGE THAT GROWS IN VALUE AS YOU APPLY IT [KEEN 2000] [SEE ABOVE CUSTOMER INPUT AND FEEDBACK]

- WITH STRATEGIC ALLIANCES RESPOND YOUR MARKET AND REACH OUT TO POTENTIAL CUSTOMERS ; [SEE INTERNATIONAL COMPETITION TRADE POLICY ABOVE]

//

page 73: Electronic Business Systems Modern Enterprise: Design Manage and Lead

WEB CONCEPTS :

- URL (Universal Resource Locator);

- HTTP (Hypertext Transfer Protocol):

- HTML (Hypertext Markup Language):

- Firewalls:

- Web enabling languages and software:

- Markup and SGML (Standard Generalised Markup Language)

- HTML

- HTML tags

- Dynamic HTML (DHTML)

//

REFERENCES / BIBLIOGRAPHY

Mousavi, A (2008):Electronic Business Systems Modern Enterprise Design Manage and Lead pub: Brunel University Press

page 121 - 122: Electronic Business Systems Modern Enterprise, Design Manage and Lead;

//

CHAPTER 3

POLICY AND THE SOCIAL SCIENCES AND LITERATURE

SEMIOTICS, TEXTUAL ANALYSIS

> We can therefore imagine a *science which would study the life of signs within society...* We call it semiology, form the Greek *semion* ['sign']. It would teach us what signs consist of, what laws govern them. Since it does not yet exist we cannot say what it will be, but it has a right to existence; its place is assured in advance. [in Fiske, 1990 : 51/2]

The framework of semiotics can be summarised into three main areas of study as follows :

- **The sign itself**. the study of different signs, of the different way that these signs convey meaning, and of the way they relate to the people who use them. For signs are human constructs and can only be understood in terms of the uses people put them to.
- The codes or systems into which signs are organised; **to which the sign refers**. It covers the ways that codes have developed in order to meet the needs of a society or culture, or to exploit the channels of communication available for their transmission.

The culture which codes and signs operate; **the users of the sign**. This depends on the use of these codes and signs for its own existence and form. [Fiske, 1990 : 40]

Semiotic analysis between two different types of meaning.

'Denotation' is the 'first order' of signification generated by the 'signifier' and the signified [Chandler, WWW]; the initial, common-sense and obvious meaning of the sign [Fiske, 1990 : 85]. Hall [cited in Chandler, WWW] regards this as the 'literal' meaning of a sign.

'Connotation', refers to the 'second order' of signification. Hall calls it the 'associative' meaning, the interaction that occurs when a sign meets the feelings or emotions of the users and the values of their culture [Fiske, 1990 : 86]. For Pierce 'connotation' is divided into three more subtle types of sign, as follows : *iconic* sign, as one that resembles the 'signified'; *symbolic* sign, as one depending on individual connotation; *indexical* sign, as one having associations and inherent connections.

Barthes [1977], illustrate the difference between denotation and connotation, in medium of photography. He sees 'denotation' as the mechanical reproduction on film of the object at which the camera is pointing. He sees 'connotation', on the other hand, as the individualised aspect of the process - the selection of what to include in the frame, the use of focus, camera angle, lighting etc.

'Denotation' becomes the term for *what* is being photographed, while 'Connotation' refers to *how* it is being captured on film [Fiske : 1990 : 86].

The concept of *'codes'* set of principles that are dynamic. Codes are difficult to perceive because they are characteristically pervasive, specific and clear-cut, to a point where they are almost invisible [Boyd-Barrett, 1987 : 150]. They are historically and socio-culturally situated, and further divide into two sub-categories - the *broadcast* code, in which the audience is wider and cliché is more obviously employed, and the *narrowcast* code, in which the audience is more limited since the principles used are more subtle [Chandler, WWW].

'Intertextuality', a concept first introduced by the post-structuralist Julia Kristeva [Chandler, WWW], is also a consideration, since it is the norm that media texts should exist in relation to others. It is therefore reasonable, as Thomas Sebeok suggests, to accept the value of semiotics as :

> The pivotal branch of the integrated science of communication ... concerned with the formulation and encoding of messages by sources, the transmission of these messages through channels, the decoding and interpretation of these messages by destinations, and their signification. [in Blonsky, 1985 : 451]

In the world of advertising, there is continuous pressure to create adverts that are increasingly more in the image of audience motives and desires. so there is a need to include audience experience within the adverts [McLuhan, 1964 : 226]. Fiske [1990 : 103] stresses that advertisers take advantage of the technical scope of photography to 'insert' or 'superimpose' objects in one syntagm onto another, to create something new and imaginatively striking.

The fuctions of expectation of a reward from the product is the primary basis for effect, though as McQuail observes [1987 : 294] there may be other bases for appeal, such as symbolic coercion [appeal to fear or anxiety], referent power [endorsement by stars etc.], authority [use by experts], and even appeals to deeper psychological motivations. Ray [1973], cited in McQuail, believes there is generally a balance between the processes of cognition, attitude formation and behaviour change, though this balance may be variable.

The underlying philosophy behind advertising is commercial – to make money through displaying the product e.g. tv commercials or print media inviting the viewer to part with their money.

The genre of advertising implies the practices of buying and selling in an economic market situation either monopoly barrier to competitive market from entering the market, or competitive mass market of generic imitations of a monopoly brand.

Advertising discourses or debates enable audiences to negotiate the roles of consumer, employee and citizen. As Jensen [1995 : 66] stresses, there is historical research available that documents this multi-step semiosis of advertising, circulating commodities as well as conceptions of society, derived from the work of Barthes [1957/73], Berger [1972], and Schudson [1984]. As Jensen points that Raymond Williams and Michael Schudson refer to advertising as constitutive of a widespread cultural practice of politics that are views , viewpoints and values of justice and fairness - the art of capitalism as a valued politics[Williams, 1992] and 'capitalism's way of saying "I love you" to itself' [Schudson, 1984]. McLuhan [1964 : 230] that the Graphic Revolution (technology revolution) has shifted our culture away from the private ideals of 'point-of-view' corporate images (point of view corporate images like fordism, mass market, hypodermic needle broadcasting to the mass as a whole and achieving a desired effect – fordism slogan ' you can have any car as long as it is black' mass production manufacturing factories), in that photographs and television seduce us to the more complex world of the group icon (niche market, appealing to selective individuals, flexible specialization, post-fordism).. Fiske [1990 : 93] also notes that there is now a move towards more surrealist, metaphorical advertising.

/,,,,,,,,,,,,,,,,,,,,,,,,,,,,,,,,,,,,,,,/

In Summary, Semiology, Semiotics:

- the sign—that is, something that stands for something else;
- the sign is made up of: a *signifier* and the *signified;*
- the *signifier* is the thing that points to an underlying meaning (the term *sign vehicle* is sometimes used instead of *signifier);*
- the *signified* is the meaning to which the signifier points;
- a denotative meaning is the manifest or more obvious meaning of a signifier and as such indicates its function;
- a sign function is an object that denotes a certain function;
- a connotative meaning is a meaning associated with a certain social context that is in addition to its denotative meaning;
- *polysemy* refers to a quality of signs—namely, that they are always capable of being interpreted in many ways;
- the *code* is the generalized meaning that interested parties may seek to instil in a sign; a code is sometimes also called a *sign system.*

Semiotics is the hidden meanings that reside in texts. For example, the curriculum vitae (CV) or employment CV, contains such features as: personal details; education; previous and current posts; administrative responsibilities and experience; teaching experience; research experience; research grants acquired; and publications. We can treat the CV as a system of interlocking 'signifiers' that signify 'denotative' meaning a summary of the individual's experience (its sign function) and at the 'connotative level' gives a perception, an indication the individual's value, or worth in employment.

Semiotic or Textual Analysis of a CV				
Sign = what it is	**Signifier** = meaning of it, underlying meaning or purpose	**Signified** =- meaning to which signifier points	**Denotation** = what it shows	**Connotation** = meaning associated with it, what it symbolises
CV or Curriculum Vitae	Underlying purpose/meaning of a CV is to	Points to Employment, Career, Work,	CV shows Personal details,	CV indicates or symbolises employee's value that is connected

		education or	with the employment i.e.
gain employment, to be employed	Job	previous emplyment listed on CV	education (in denotation) shows that the employee is qualified for the employment

CHAPTER 3

POLICY AND THE SOCIAL SCIENCES AND LITERATURE

POLICY

Outline Bell's and Castells' research on the 'information society'.
What would you need to consider in evaluating their research? Answer ' Work'

Definition of Work

In defining the term 'work', it could be argued that it is not a simple term to define. This is because some theorists such as Keith Grint (1991) see work as being in employment (participating in paid work). However tasks undertaken by people in employment (paid work such as Cleaning or Childcare) are also untaken by those who are not employed (unpaid work). Additionally, work crosses over to leisure and hence one could consider work as a leisure activity. For instance some people like myself enjoy playing tennis at their leisure whilst others play tennis because it is their employment (paid work).

There are also the changing patterns of work. In pre-industrial societies, Grint observes that work was seen as a 'necessity' rather than 'free' will/choice and so was frowned upon and considered as work undertaken by slaves.

However with industrialisation (with the industrial revolution - changes in modes of production in Britain since the mid-18th century from Agriculture to power-driven machinery), employers were able to impose regular work patterns on employees such as working to time.

Also, for Karl Marx (1844) this meant 'alienated labour'. This being work alienating workers so that workers are unable to express themselves (by being creative and working to their own time like traditional craftsmen) in their work and so are isolated from themselves and other workers – as a result of people competing to get employment in the labour market. Marx examined this ('alienated labour') in terms of Capitalist Infrastructure. From my knowledge, the Capitalist Bourgeoisie (rising elite minority of middle class) own the means of production (the factories) and the workers (proletariat) do not own or have control over the commodities/goods they produce and are treated as commodities themselves because in the same way the cost of commodities are assessed, their wages and 'wage labour' depends on the Supply and Demand the market (market forces) of and they could find themselves laid off (jobless) if demand is low. Hence the capitalist were profitable because their exploited the workers by extracting 'surplus value' (the difference between the value of the work undertaken and the wages paid).

Nonetheless, in the 'Information Society' (INFORMATION SOCIETY SYNONYMOUS WITH Post-Fordist / Post-Industrial / Network / Knowledge Society), Shoshana Zuboff (1988 writes that *"workers now controlled the production process through manipulating abstract symbols on computer screens"* (Zuboff, 1988: p130). Here Zuboff's point is that with ICT, 'intellectual skills' are replacing some 'redundant manual skills' (**deskilling**: use of less skilled labour since work was broken down into simpler task along Fordist assembly lines or employing worker operated machines). This greatly increases the amount of information available to both workers and managers. Here managers can choose to use ICT to 'informate the workplace': spread information; challenge or reinforce traditional hierarchies; or monitor employees like one could observe in the Film 'Charlie Chaplin Modern Times' reeled at Residential School (Chichester Theatre) on Monday 23rd July 2007.

Furthermore, Manufacturers use ICTs to manufacture goods to the principles of **"flexible specialization"** (Mackay et al, 2001, p15). Here this increases the skills needed by the workforce because machines can be re-programmed to perform

166

different tasks so that goods are no longer 'mass-produced' like in Fordism along 'assembly lines' but produced for a niche market (individual market) that caters for the individual life-style needs of the consumer. With Post-Fordism (period since late 1980s onwards characterised by Consumer Society), the Japanese *"just-in-time delivery"* (Mackay et al, 2001, p14) system had been adopted. 'Just-in-time' works on the basis that rather than like in Fordism where goods were held in stock, in Post-Fordism, the computer tells when stocks are running low and stocks are delivered just before they are needed.

Also in the Information Society, domestic work (unpaid work in the household) is no longer the only work carried out in the home. Home work (paid work carried out in the home for an external employer) forms work undertaken in the home. Such homework will involve Telework (working from home using information technology). Teleworkers include consultants, designers (like graphic designer Joan Salmer, shown **in the video 'BBC Newsnight' dated 21 February 2000 in Session 2 residential school),** writers and those carrying out routine secretarial, clerical or sales work away from the city office.

Additionally, in the Information Society, there has been a rise in information-service based occupations (discussed in Bell). Similarly part time (paid) work has grown substantially since the 1951 from 4% of workers to 21% in 2001 and 93% of women made up the numbers in part-time work in 2001 (Social Trends, 2002, p71). Also, the part-time work are undertaken by workers with childcare responsibilities – those who have dependants as noted in the Metro newspaper (19 May 2007).

In the Information Society, employment has shifted from manufacturing to service occupation (see Bell) and no longer job security/job for life since the type of work offered is mostly contract work rather than permanent work.

Nevertheless, from the twentieth Century, Fordist manufacturing industries emerged to provide the mass-consumer goods such as cars, fridges, televisions and washing machines to be used during unpaid 'non-work' time. Here the consumption of goods and services during leisure 'non-work' time had begun and is a major feature in Post-Fordism/Information Society. Also one person's leisure provides another person employment. For instance, one person's leisure might consist of [listening to Ipod, downloading music and audio-visual from the internet, interacting with one's Sky/Cable TV by freezing, using close-ups and finding out background information of TV programmes, uploading games consoles such as **Nintendo** to the internet to play games with other players in i.e. United Kingdom, United States and Japan. This leisure activity provides another person with employment such as those workers that **manufacture** the new technology/ICT products.

Bibliography

Grint, K (1991) 'The Sociology of Work: An Introduction", Polity Press, Cambridge.

Metro Newspaper (19 May 2007), 'Two Million swap a career for Caring

Zuboff, S. (1988) 'In the Age of the Smart Machine', Basic Books, New York.

Social Trends, 2002 (2002), ed. J.Church (London: HMSO)

CHAPTER 3

POLICY AND THE SOCIAL SCIENCES AND LITERATURE

POLICY

Why has Media Policy become such a central issue of political concern?

Media Policy is the government's policy paper documents on the regulation of media industries and structures, and the agency of free will of its viewers consumers.

Industries refers to radio, television, web telecoms, press industries.

Structures – refers to rules and ways of regulating practices that 'constrain' 'restrict' the fairness of viewers or deemed a threat over the behaviour of free individuals of the viewers, economic structures of Monopolies and politicians wanting free market, competitive market of more than one media companies giving consumers more choice on competitive price and competitive programming for instance.

Media Policy has become central issue in politics because the growth in new information communication technologies, such as the web's combination of audio, visual and textual broadcasting, Have more than one media, medium which has divided the politics of those politicians in power who create laws on regulating structures in society for the common good, who seek to control the media as one mass Hypodermic needle for one desired effect of achieving public good.

Firstly the civil servants either adhoc or select committees involved in the decision making of media policy are divided on views within the medium, media policy report, the peacock report, the Beveridge Committee Report (a media policy initiative) was said to have influenced the shape of commercial broadcasting companies because of its suggestion of 'spot adverts' as opposed to 'sponsored programmes' in order to give advertisers less control and more liberty to consumers the viewers as they would be able to consume for gratification and the use of it rather than influencing the control over the behaviours of which can influence a negative outcome eg in child viewers their behaviours towards bullying and violence on TV eg 'chucky' in 'child's play' was an intrinsic aid towards the Jamie Bulger case, trial back in 1993, and playground violence after a viewing of power rangers 1995.

The Broadcasting Act 1990 (a media policy) such to reduce the power the Independent Broadcasting Authority (a government policy initiative set up to regulate broadcasting media) has over commercial TV and thus power over the liberty of consumers what they want to watch and how they react, (less control over the hypodermic needle behaviour of consumers, the hypodermic needle theory that viewers follow what they see on TV). Although the Act did allow British Satellite Broadcasting (public corporation owned by Rupert Murdoch) merge with Sky Channel for a monopoly,

However, new information communication technologies - one combined medium on the web has made media companies more powerful, examples have included napster providing free music download s, the power of Microsoft has to buy or own 50 per cent of the market share of its os operating system monopoly creating a barrier to entry for smaller competitor to come into the market and offer consumers more choice in competitive prices, other channels etc.

Former Prime Minister, Margaret Thatcher, took a conservative 'new right' which is a liberal approach of strong state of what Liberal John Locke terms as protecting freedom and national interest of citizens / electorate (voters) and minimal government in market, allowing media companies to regualting freely of government control.

New Labour under the directions of former Prime Minister Tony Blair once said ' if you do not see the internet as an opportunity, it will be a threat. In two years time the internet could be as common place in the office as the telephone, if you are not exploiting the opportunities of a commerce you could go bankrupt'.

e.g. Successful competitively priced Amazon Digital and struggling in affordable Jessops digital cameras under owner entrepreneur Peter Jones' pitch to Sky News Thursday 28 March 2013, opening new stores in London's west end following it stores going into administration in early 2012.

Tony Blair speech has now being fulfilled, however observing the effect of media as a central issue of concern to policy makers / politics, the convergence of such media can have consequences, demising Thatcher gov't the minimal government in the free market, here the media companies and recent govt concern over press regulation.

Hutchinson (1999) observed that "globalisation imposes substantial constraints on the Economic power governments, [to keep place with convergence of media companies] so advances in technology affects regulation authority" p63 namely phone hacking of the News Of The World, former Sunday tabloid
mid-market newspaper owned by Rupert Murdoch and the Leveson Inquiry (2012), a media policy inquiry, for a press regulation authority over traditionally free press industry to curtail media structures having more power than the government to protect public good, public interest.

The Communications White Paper (2000) another policy initiative to come out of media policy, provided the foundations in regulating broadcasting.

In the governments view and as Curran and Seaton explains 'broadcasting was also viewed as a being a powerful influence
that needed to be harnessed to the public good". (323)

The Communications White Paper's aim was to allow more competition powers of smaller competitive media providers in order to regulate the media market economy, the monopoly market barrier for the competitors of BskyB's rate card review through the use of EPG, (electronic programme guides).

Reference, bibliography, extrinsic aids, intrinsic aids:

- Broadcasting Publication 15 Dec 2000

- Coxall and Robins Contemporary British Politics (1998) pub Macmillan.

- Curran and Seaton (1997) Power without Reponsibilty

- Grossberg, Wartella and Whitney (1998) Media Making Mass Media Popular Culture

- Hutchinson (1999) Media Policy an introduction, pub Blackwell (1999), Metro newspaper 6 Jan. 2001.

- Stuart Price (1998) Media Policy

CHAPTER 3

POLICY AND THE SOCIAL SCIENCES AND LITERATURE

POLICY

'In the recent past, social structures largely shaped human behaviour, but now individuals have great opportunities to shape their own lives'.

Do you agree with this statement? Draw on at least THREE blocks of D to your answer.

Social structures include Language, Science, Modern political ideologies and Ethnicity (discussed below) that limits or influences the opportunities that individuals have to shape their own lives. Whereas Agency refers to the ability individuals have to act independently and to make their own free choices. In the past, periods in society such as Modernity and Fordism (discussed below) largely shaped human behaviour. However, in Post-modernity (late 1980s onwards discussed below) and Post-Fordism (period since late 1980s onwards characterised by Consumer Society, discussed below) individuals now have agency (great opportunities) to shape their own lives. This is discussed further in the essay with reference to three blocks: Block 7; Block 1 and Block 5.

In Block 7, 07, Rational Choice Theory and Crime:

From my studies in Block 7, the idea of Rational Choice Theory (RCT) is that autonomous individual actors (acting on their own using their own free will, in the liberal sense) act on their self interest and are therefore calculating. Calculating is a borrowed paradigm/model or feature of the *'economic man'* in Economics who simply seeks to maximise his or her utility and therefore will calculate his purchases in light of his/her tastes for products and the relative prices of those products[1].

---

[1]   Collins Dictionary of Economics

Nonetheless, according to Encarta, 'Crime' can be defined as a 'public wrong'. Crime can be distinguished into seven main types and 'crime against property' (one of the seven types) will be my focal point for RCT.

In relation to the past, crime (such as what constitutes crime, its definition and accepted aetiology (cause) was largely seen a social problem (social structures that affect the individual's **human behaviour** from being rational and able to think for themselves). This idea of crime as a social problem (social structure) led Scientists to claim that the origins of crime (particularly when proving a guilty mind – **mens rea**) could be traced to: individuals growing up in a dysfunctional family unit (Structural explanations 2: Families[2]); hereditary / in the genes passed down from parents (Structural explanations 1: Biology[3]); neurological disorders or genetic defects in the brain like in the case of the mentally ill (Structural explanations 1: Biology[4]); or individuals being part of external agencies such as gangs that have an influence on them and their ability to think rationally (Structural explanations 2: Culture[5]).

However in view of Rational Choice Theory (RCT) that individuals have great opportunities to shape their own lives one could argue that in recent years as emphasised on bbc.co.uk/news report on Monday 23 October 2006 *"there has been a dramatic rise in the number of people who own* [property – main feature of 'consumer society' discussed below - such as] *a mobile phone and in parallel with this there has been a rise in the number of thefts"*.

In addition, recorded crime rates (such as those processed through an administrative system (i.e. Victim Support National Office[6]) or an enforcement agency (i.e. Metropolitan Police) or Investigator (i.e. Home Office) are socially constructed and therefore some crime especially theft in the workplace **(white collar crimes)** go unreported. This is because those sorts of crime are **"hidden crimes"** and can only be

---

2   Mooney et al, 2004, D Introductory Chapter p31
3   Mooney et al, 2004, D Introductory Chapter p29
4   Mooney et al, 2004, D Introductory Chapter p29
5   Mooney et al, 2004, D Introductory Chapter p33
6   Victim Support National Office has branches in Oval SW11, England and Wales, Northern Ireland, Republic of Ireland and Scotland. It is an independent charity that helps people cope with the effects of crime and they provide free and confidential support and information to help one deal with their experiences.

proved through evidence such as a witness or having recordings on Closed Circuit Television (CCTV), and some theft in the workplace are not usually noticed or seen until someone notices or realises something has gone missing. An example of this took place in the two companies I previously worked for where the same items namely a laptop was stolen.

Here the perpetrators were not caught and this therefore supports RCT as whoever stole these two laptops knew how **to shape their own lives**: they knew how to maximise their utility and avoid pain of a fine and imprisonment. Theft in the work place accounts to the maximum penalty of £5,000.00 fine and/or 6 months imprisonment[7] – this is a hefty punishment and these individuals that stole the laptops knew how to avoid this.

In Block 1, 01, Identity:

Ethnicization (according to Woodward, 2004: p125) is the *"dynamic processes that construct people as belonging to a particular 'ethnic' group on the basis of assumptions about culture, national origin, or language"*. This was the case at School when an Indian pupil from Kenya – East Africa (I know) stated that he was going back home on holiday to Africa and the whole class (whom are predominantly white) automatically assumed he was going to Ghana because that was the only African Country they knew. Today, this is no longer the case because we now live in an **'information society'** and **'knowledge society'** where news information in the media on multi-cultural neighbourhoods including Notting Hill Carnival has created an awareness of different ethnic groups and cultures in society.

Similarly, **Racialization** (coined by Ali Rattansi) is where social structures (i.e. **in language**: literature, books – visual text through the representation of images and narrative) try to represent group differences in terms of **biological 'race'** (inherent physical features) rather than **cultural ethnicity** (non-white cultures like particular

---

[7]   Mooney et al, 2004, D Introductory Chapter p5

173

kinds of music like Hip-Hop or food - exotic/ethnic food i.e. plantain or yam as oppose to 'fish and chips' which is not considered ethnic). Thus this makes 'race' *"socially, economically and psychologically significant"* (according to Woodward, 2004: p125). For example, the **Tar baby advertising campaigns of the 1950s** by soap manufacturers showed black people as resembling the colour of tar with big pink/red lips and wide eyes, with a slogan suggesting that if black people used the soap produced by these manufacturers, they would be fair in skin like their white counterparts.

In the media today (in **post-modernity**) advertising campaigns tend to be specialised towards the needs of individuals in a multi-cultural society (individual life-style) rather than targeting groups in society based on 'loose' stereotypes on 'biological race'. For instance, the tropical juice 'Rhythm' imported from Jamaica in the Caribbean shows cultural forms of ethnicity such as exotic fruits used to make the juice like Pineapple or Mango to name a few. The same can be said for Hip Hop music or Rap music. Hip-Hop/Rap music developed in the late 1970s out of black communities in South Bronx and Brooklyn districts of New York (in North America) and alongside saw the onset of a whole range of Rap fashion that were being popularised. For instance, baseball caps, sweatshirts, break dancing and roller skates. Today (evidently on Youtube.com music site), Hip-Hop is not just music associated with Black individuals alone, it is now an international phenomenon not just attracting Black individuals and Hispanics in many indigenous languages, it also attracts Caucasians, particularly middle-class Caucasians such as BBC's Radio 1 DJs like Tim Westwood who presents Radio 1 every Saturday from 9pm to 12am).

Alongside, in terms of Identity, Hip-Hop music is now part of today's youth 'popular' culture whereby youths have economic power (money to spend on Rap fashion, and entertainment such as Music CDs) and a desire to be markedly different from both children and adults in dress, language and behaviour. Hip-Hop offers them this **Agency - opportunities to shape their own lives (Identity) such as being** Individual or different from other age groups in society.

In Block 5, 05, Knowledge and Social Change:

From my studies in Block 5, my understanding is that in the past, **Fordism** (period immediately after World War II characterised by mass production of the same thing like black cars) **shaped human behaviours**. This is because individuals did not have agency to choose, their choice was largely dictated by social structures (industrialisation and society). Here individuals had to have what their neighbours had and could not choose to buy goods that would make them individual from their neighbours since goods where made on a mass scale.

However, in recent times this has changed. Post-Fordism (late 1980s onwards) encourages **'flexible specialization'** whereby products are designed and individualised to the consumers' needs (niche products) and Post-Modernity (late 1980s onwards) characterised by global manufacturing/globalization and new service industry/customer service. In Post-Fordism and Post-Modernity, the theory of **'consumer society'** can also help to explain how individuals have agency (great opportunities) to shape their own lives. Consumer Society is where consumers have more knowledge (**'knowledge society'**) about products and services and are encouraged to consume/purchase more and where consumers value limited/niche produced goods that make them stand out as individuals.

Here **social change** (towards a **consumer society**) reflects *"a broader decline in trust in traditional sources of knowledge and expertise"* (Goldblatt, 2004: p140) such as modern political ideology (social structure that limit the opportunities individuals have to shape their own lives) in Modernity (from eighteenth century that rejected religious authority/ **knowledge** in favour of modern political ideology/**knowledge**) like Liberalism that promote minimal state control in the economy ('free market' principles supported by both Conservative New Right and New Labour's Third Way) in favour of economic growth such as **Industrialisation** that has impacted on the environment causing Global Warming, Greenhouse effect, Pollution, risk to Conservation and Climate Change. Here in recent years individuals are in favour of alternative ideology/**knowledge** such as Environmental knowledge/Green thinking. For example households and offices are 'going green' (limiting the effects of i.e. Global Warming in their own lives) by recycling their rubbish as well reducing their carbon footprint by boycotting goods that have been imported. This **shifts power from** Producers selling what they make to *"producing what consumers want"*

(Goldblatt, 2004: p140) and for example consumers can boycott supermarkets that produce more carbon emissions to the environment.

However, in saying this, one could note that with i.e. 'free view' TV /sky TV, it overstates consumers as having real power since consumers are getting more of the same thing (popular commercial television) rather than a choice. In other words (going back to Henry Ford) '[one] can have any colour as long as it is black'.

To conclude the above shows how individuals have great opportunities to shape their own lives discussed in Rational Choice Theory of Block 7 or in Block 1 with 'Identity' or 'Consumer Society' and 'Knowledge Society' in Block 5. However, particularly related to consumption (in consumer society), there are still significant social structural constraints on human behaviour whereby individuals are not getting more choice but more of the same thing. Balancing this social structural constraint against other Agency (discussed above) that individuals have today, it is evident that individuals really do have more opportunities and choices to shape their own lives than they had in the past.

Word Count
1,639 words

Bibliography

1. bbc.co.uk/new (Monday 23rd October 2006) News Article: 'Crime Support Financial: What happens if my mobile phone is stolen?'

2. Goldblatt, David (2004, 2nd Edition) D Book 5 Knowledge and the Social Sciences: Theory, Method, Practice, London, The Open University Press, p140 **(Block 5, 05)**

3. Mooney, G et al (2004, 2nd Edition) 'Introductory Chapter:- tales of fear and fascination: the crime problem in the contemporary uk', Milton Keynes, The Open University, p5, 29, 31, 33, 34 **(Block 7, 07)**

4. Rattansi, A And Westwood, S (1994) Racism, Modernity And Identity, Cambridge, Polity Press

5. Woodward, Kath (2004), 'Questioning Identity: gender, class, ethnicity', London, Open University, p125 **(Block 1, 01)**

CHAPTER 3

POLICY AND THE SOCIAL SCIENCES AND LITERATURE

POLICY

CHAPTER 3

POLICY AND THE SOCIAL SCIENCES AND LITERATURE

POLICY

Working Title: **Anti Social Behaviour is not clear cut, it depends on time and place**

youth antisocial behaviour

hoodie (seen as antisocial and results to forms of punishment - e.g. disallowed in shopping centres).

the ubiquitous image of the 'hoodie' has become a trade mark for antisocial behaviour and the hoodie bearer is assumed
to have 'trouble' on their mind.

hoodie is a social construct because locally in Britain it is seen as antisocial but
in muslim countries hoodies are allowed and seen as a form of religious garment e.g.

taliban scarf and, sari, veil, hijab scarf.

conflict theory - Commitment to social justice: labelling theory discriminates and is wrong in this case
because not all hoodies are criminals

ANTISOCIAL BEHAVIOUR, 'JUSTICE' AND CRIMINALISATION

HOW ANTISOCIAL IS 'ANTISOCIAL BEHAVIOUR?'

The term antisocial behaviour has become synonymous with 'trouble', and it is remarkable the
speed with which the term has entered our vocabulary and taken on a life of its own.
However, defining what behaviour is 'antisocial' is a rather more difficult task.
In the same way that deviance is in the eye of the beholder, so that which is 'antisocial'
is defined by the reaction of others and therefore RELATIVE (SOCIAL CONSTRUCT) TO TIME AND PLACE (LOCAL/GLOBAL).
THE cRIME AND DISORDER ACT 1998 [IMPORTANT, A POLICY DOCUMENT) defined antisocial behaviour
as that which 'which caused or was likely to cause harrassment, alarm or distress
to one or more persons not of the same household [LOCAL / GLOBAL] as himself'.
This appears deliberately vague [VAGUE], with one MP, in a now much quoted statement in the
House of Commons, likening antisocial behaviour to an elephant on the doorstep, [doorstep is LOCAL/GLOBAL]
in that it is 'easier to recognise than define' (cited in Rutherford, 2000, and MacDonald, 2006).

Key questions that will allow you to further 'unpack' your title

Anti-social behaviour depends on the Social Context (Place) and Time, e.g. certain Local and Global Relations.

This includes view that in certain local and global relations, certain forms of Behaviour are viewed as Anti-social in certain local and global social contexts, while it is viewed as a crime in others.

Similarly, in Criminology Policy Document, The Crime and Disorder Act 1998 defined 'Antisocial Behaviour' as that which 'caused or was likely to 'cause harassment, alarm or distress to one or more persons not of the same household as himself'.

The defining literature I will use to analyse my project's working title. This being **'Anti Social Behaviour is not clear cut, it depends on time and place'**

www.statewatch.org/asbo/ASBOwatch.html 'ABSOwatch' monitors the use of antisocial behaviour orders and this website provides some useful legal information and evaluation of the use of the ASBO.

www.crimeandjustice.org.uk – website for the Centre for Crime and Justice Studies

www.corporateaccountability.org – the Centre for Corporate Accountability is a charity which promotes worker and public safety, and which has been particularly active in campaigning for greater levels of accountability for deaths in the workplace.

www.nacro.org.uk – NACRO is a community agency that aims to reduce crime.

www.homeoffice.gov.uk – an invaluable source of information about current government policy on crime, antisocial behaviour and policy strategies. This website will provide me with links to research findings and Criminological policy documents, such as the Respect Action Plan, that aims to keep up to date with developments in the law and the political response to Crime and Antisocial behaviour.

How the policy has been addressed in Policy Terms

In Criminology Policy Document, The Crime and Disorder Act 1998, looking at the Social Context (Place – local and global) and Time the Anti-social behaviour had happened, it appears deliberately vague, with one much quoted MP's statement in the House of Commons, likening antisocial behaviour to an elephant on the doorstep, in that it is 'earlier to recognise than to define' (cited in Rutherford, 2000), and MacDonald, 2006).

A reference list

Rutherford (2000) and MacDonald (2006)

www.statewatch.org/asbo/ASBOwatch.html

www.crimeandjustice.org.uk

www.corporateaccountability.org

www.nacro.org.uk

www.homeoffice.gov.uk

Harradine, S., Kodz, J., Lemetti, F. and Jones, B. (2004) Defining and Measuring Anti-social Behaviour, Development and Practice Report 26, London, Home Office.

CHAPTER 3

POLICY AND THE SOCIAL SCIENCES AND LITERATURE

POLICY

Working Title: **Anti Social Behaviour is not clear cut, it depends on time and place**

Key questions that will allow you to further 'unpack' your title

Anti-social behaviour depends on the Social Context (Place) and Time, e.g. certain Local and Global Relations.

This includes view that in certain local and global relations, certain forms of Behaviour are viewed as Anti-social in certain local and global social contexts, while it is viewed as a crime in others.

Similarly, in Criminology Policy Document, The Crime and Disorder Act 1998 defined 'Antisocial Behaviour' as that which 'caused or was likely to 'cause harassment, alarm or distress to one or more persons not of the same household as himself'.

Example: Binge drinking (excessive drinking) and it's outside nightclubs (social context crimes in public places - crimes of the streets) is seen as anti-social in Britain while in the Middle East (global social context of crime) is considered a criminal offence often bearing the highest penalty.

Similarly, within Corporations (local and global social context of crime – crimes of suites) which are hidden crimes, Corporations like in Europe and USA had wine clubs which encourage (excessive drinking) while other's like in Asia e.g Japan observe and practice cultural religious traditional rituals on which their corporations were founded.

The defining literature I will use to analyse my project's working title. This being **'Anti Social Behaviour is not clear cut, it depends on time and place'**

www.statewatch.org/asbo/ASBOwatch.html 'ABSOwatch' monitors the use of antisocial behaviour orders and this website provides some useful legal information and evaluation of the use of the ASBO.

www.crimeandjustice.org.uk – website for the Centre for Crime and Justice Studies

www.corporateaccountability.org – the Centre for Corporate Accountability is a charity which promotes worker and public safety, and which has been particularly active in campaigning for greater levels of accountability for deaths in the workplace.

www.nacro.org.uk – NACRO is a community agency that aims to reduce crime.

www.homeoffice.gov.uk – an invaluable source of information about current government policy on crime, antisocial behaviour and policy strategies. This website will provide me with links to research findings and Criminological policy documents, such as the Respect Action Plan, that aims to keep up to date with developments in the law and the political response to Crime and Antisocial behaviour.

How the policy has been addressed in Policy Terms

In Criminology Policy Document, The Crime and Disorder Act 1998, looking at the Social Context (Place – local and global) and Time the Anti-social behaviour had happened, it appears deliberately vague, with one much quoted MP's statement in the House of Commons, likening antisocial behaviour to an elephant on the doorstep, in that it is 'earlier to recognise than to define' (cited in Rutherford, 2000), and MacDonald, 2006).

A reference list

Rutherford (2000) and MacDonald (2006)

www.statewatch.org/asbo/ASBOwatch.html

www.crimeandjustice.org.uk

www.corporateaccountability.org

www.nacro.org.uk

www.homeoffice.gov.uk

Harradine, S., Kodz, J., Lemetti, F. and Jones, B. (2004) Defining and Measuring Anti-social Behaviour, Development and Practice Report 26, London, Home Office.

CHAPTER 3

POLICY AND THE SOCIAL SCIENCES AND LITERATURE

POLICY

The course Welfare Crime and Society is about two aspects, on the one hand you have Social Policy (Welfare) and on the other hand you have Crime / Criminology (Crime Control).

Thus welfare policies have both welfare, and crime control elements – like a double edge sword

Key to Social Policy / Social Justice is Welfare Policies aimed at bringing about welfare / well being.

Key to Crime / Criminology / Crime Justice is Crime Policies and Criminal Justice System who punishes offenders / deviance / antisocial behaviour / criminals.

The same policies targeted at the disadvantage groups to increase their welfare and wellbeing, are the same policies aimed at (crime / social) control on these disadvantage groups.

Example, Welfare to Work Policies aim to find unemployed (disadvantaged) people jobs (welfare aspects) and at the same time if they do not want to find a job, their benefits are stopped (crime control aspect) – shows entanglement between Welfare and Crime Control

CHAPTER 3

POLICY AND THE SOCIAL SCIENCES AND LITERATURE

POLICY

Social Justice could be defined as having fairness and having equal worth as a citizen. Social Justice is also about alleviating poverty, its about social inclusion and social well-being.

However, Social Injustice could be defined as a individual, citizen or group experiencing poverty, inequality, social exclusion and harm.

Social Justice is a contested meaning (discussed below) and is changing through groups mobilised to act against Social Injustices in order to bring about change promoting Social Justice. Such include Black people and Coloured people of former Apartheid South Africa (mobilised against) the **system of Apartheid in Government**

public policy racially segregated public services such as public toilets, schools, neighbourhoods and shops.

The relationship between Social Justice and Crime Control is Crime control policies used to address social injustices to bring about Social Justice through Corrective Justice (which in tort law is a remedy for wrongful harms / civil wrongs or punishment upon violation of legal entitlements such as benefits). Such include the Work Place Act that aims to eradicate Social harm (or social ills, crime **or death as in the tragic case of the Chinese Cockle-Pickers depicted in the film 'Ghosts' in Newman et al 2008**) in the work place, or having work-related benefits withdrawn if unemployed Claimants failed to help themselves to find work – discussed below)..

The relationship between Social Justice and Social Welfare is Social Welfare policies in the form of social welfare services and provisions used to address social injustice to bring about Social Justice. Such Social Welfare services and provisions are achieved through 'Distributive Justice' where by financial resources are re-distributed through progressive taxation (taxes increase as income increase) to encourage social inclusion as redistributive resources enable poorer households to participate fully in society (or community to bring about social equality), through e.g. welfare to work policy initiatives discussed below.

Since the former Prime Minister Tony Blair, **New Labour** and it's Third Way Social Welfare policies have equated Social Justice to the 'equal worth of all citizens' through **recognition**.

Symbolic = representation

Recognition as a form of Social Justice refers to respect and representation or symbolic of creed such as Gender, Race, Sexuality, Disability and Physical differences.

Thus **Mis-recognition as a form of Social Injustice** refer to lack of respect and **mis-representation of certain groups through which harm is caused** to these groups such as the largely black, poor, deprived and impoverished victims (experiencing social inequality and thus seen as problem population in terms of need of welfare and crime control) of the Hurricane Katrina Disaster in New Orleans in year 2005 whose conditions was mis-managed by the **United States Authorities** and so they were left to experience the full force of the Hurricane 'social' disaster, while their richer largely white neighbours had the financial resources to flee the Hurricane floods disaster.

New Labour's Third Way Social Welfare Policies see An individual's worth and recognition (having Social Justice) could be seen in terms of their engagement in paid work, because participating in paid work is not only an indication of being a Citizen, but also an indication of an individual's **equal** worth in contributing to the Economic output and growth of a Society.

New Labour's Third Way Social Welfare policies to promote social Justice have been about prevention of social inequality through **self-empowering individuals (responsibilisation of individuals) by given them a 'hand up' not a 'hand-out'** (Newman et al, 2008)

Self empowerment here is making individuals take control of their own life and decisions affecting them, and making them responsible for their own welfare. This self-empowerment have been enabled through the welfare provisions of opportunities (capabilities or work capabilities in this case to enable individuals to participate fully in society through 'welfare-to-work' policy initiatives centred around 'New Deal' that provide one-to-one support with New Deal Adviser at a Job Centre Plus Government Employment Agency, work-relating training and education, and clothing grant allowance for work). These work capabilities allow individuals to build their capacities. Capacity Building has been about allowing individuals to build Human Capital such as skills, talent and abilities required for work to make use of the (work) opportunities available to them.

Building capabilities and, building capacities (human and social capital)

Self empowerment – need a hand up not a handout – see Social justice course book.

Nonetheless, a punitive and coercive (forceful) dimensions to Social Justice have also been adopted by New Labour. This is that individuals on e.g. Job Seeker's Allowance who are able to work but who fail to help themselves (self-empowerment) to look for work will have their benefits withdrawn to force such individuals to look for work (as they will be seen as not fulfilling the work requirement conditions).

Social Justice has contested meanings because Social Welfare policies and practices designed to promote Social Justice can also be a source of Social Injustice

Social Justice has contested Meanings because Social Welfare policies and practices designed to promote Social Justice can also be a source of Social Injustice for certain kinds of people. Ideas of Social Justice and Injustice developed in societies whereby Public policies and practices designed to address Social Justice to a group of people, of which the same public policies have been a source of Social Injustice to other groups of people.

A social policy issue of Social Injustice (Social injustice from the point of view of the claimant) here is that such public policies such as the 'Welfare-to-Work' policies are rule based which has punitive conditions attached to it, this condition being that if Job Seekers (Claimants of work-related benefits) are not seen as actively seeking work, their benefits are withdrawn / stopped – they are then stigmatised – it blames the victim as the cause of their own social problem or predicament of being unemployed. Whereas as Bauman 1998 in Newman et al (2008) points out, Normal Society's (social structures and institutions that limit the (work) opportunities available to such groups) brought about the Injustices in the first place.

CHAPTER 3

POLICY AND THE SOCIAL SCIENCES AND LITERATURE

POLICY

Surveillance defined as continuous observation of the behaviour of people. (Narrator – Alan Cochrane).

Surveillance = 2 definitions:

(1) Surveillance = watches over (controls through monitoring offenders so that others may be protected)

(2) Surveillance watches out for (safeguard) people and protects them.

DVD 1

Narrator Esther Saraga,

Surveillance = protective and disciplinary aspects, on the one hand = care, a kindly eye watching OUT for people. On the other hand = Deterrent or Suspicious eye watching over people, as a way of protecting people and controlling crime.

A welfare form of surveillance - The Shopping Centre at the edge of Leeds (in DVD1, Chapter 1 Introducing Surveillance) uses Closed Circuit TV (CCTV) cameras and a police officer on site. This promises safety and security to the vulnerable such as children and the elderly at risk of becoming victims of crime. For instance, Nasim notes that although there is a *"park in front of* [her] *house",* she feels much *"safer"* walking (mall walking) through the Shopping Centre.

A crime control form of surveillance - would be that offenders are responsible for their crime (an act punishable by law) and that punishing young offenders is important. The Shopping Centre partly adopted this approach to continue to remain a 'safe haven' for vulnerable people by keeping some groups out such as youths in hoodies, large groups of youths of more than five or six and trouble makers.

Also, shopping centre <u>socially excludes the poor</u> who live close by not because they are criminals but because they cannot afford to shop in the shopping centre.

Crucially, it is not always easy to separate these aspects (of Social Welfare and of Crime Control, it may be both at the same time or different things for different people

DVD illustrates tension sand welfare entanglements between WELFARE, CRIME and SOCIETY

DVD Chapter 1 = illustrates Surveillance in the every day setting of White Rose Shopping Centre, and shows the ambiguities and tensions with Surveillance. Also raises issues such as a Community of Shoppers (e.g. White Rose Learning Centre) and of borders that are managed

DVD Chapter 2 – Safeguarding Children, might be seen initially as Watching Out for and Welfare, also takes the form of collecting information that might enable social services in the prevention of harm to children or the disciplining and policing of parents – Story of Michelle formerly a drug addict and in an abusive relationship (in a violent relationship with her partner whom she wanted to escape from therefore also becoming a lone parent – lone parents can be a cause of concern to social services). She says Social Services (who are both Social Welfare systems and Criminal Justice / Crime Control Systems) make a lot of decisions without you knowing she did not know that her Son was being "removed off me" taken of her until two days before Court. Michelle recounts that when Social Workers came round, they always seem to have a note pad (a form of surveillance - monitoring and collecting information to prevent harm of children and discipline or police parents as discussed above) and she has never spoken to a Social Worker without her comments being written down (a form of monitoring). In Michelle's account, she recounts that she was scared to cough the wrong way, you will find it will be taken in the wrong way (when jotted down on the note pad), and used against you (her). Michelle also recounts that because of past experiences, some people resent someone watching you or monitoring you or assessing you but realistically Social Services can-not safeguard a child because the Mother might not one someone knocking on their door three days a week if there has been problems in the past, again you (Social Services) have to do it in the right way – Social Services have to be sensitive when you are asking someone to have to put their whole life on show including in Court etc. Michelle has experienced the harsher end of being watched OVER (Crime Control aspect) in order that (as she acknowledges herself) for her child to be Watched OUT for (Safeguarded – Social Welfare aspect) This shows that Social Welfare cannot be separated from Crime Control.

Collecting information = form of surveillance

DVD Chapter 3 – Gated Communities – tensions and entanglements between Social Welfare and Crime Control are particularly clear. On the one hand a gated community offers people Welfare in the form of Person / Community Security (images of children freely playing outside without fear of crime). A set of border and boundaries within which they can look after themselves and their family (Social Welfare). At the same time the Gates (which controlled access of phone entry system to control who can come in and CCTV to monitor who comes in, in terms of crime control) are intended to keep out undesirables (Crime control aspect). So both welfare and crime control aspects of Surveillance are apparent.

Sarah Neal – Gated community appear to offer a desire and sense of belonging, sense of togetherness and this idea has been accentuated in the contemporary political time, because of a decline in trust, a rise in insecurity, a sense of precariousness [extreme dangerousness, dangerously insecure or unstable; perilous/danger; depending on the intention of another] a growth in social fear and anxiety and think that it is a transnational kind of mood that precariousness and in that context, community with all its good associations becomes much more intense. And on the other hand, you see Gated Communities as a response to that precariousness (images showing: through, gates, cctv, phone entry system), a response to people's sense of insecurity (sign showing Community Safety, CCTV in operation 020 7 278 4444, their worries about social disorder. We could understand gating as **social retreat** as well as a search for more socialness. Through this example, Sarah Neal describes Gated Communities as a search for Social retreat and more socialness (Social Welfare. We again see the entanglement between Welfare concerns and the control of Crime).

DVD Chapter 4 – Migrant Border Control - (Migrant border control). Here borders are crucial and they are the central focus of border control and migrants. Here it might seem that surveillance is primarily watching over and excluding and monitoring undesirables (those that have not entered legally – immigrants and terrorists see Review DVD Community)

One Spanish Border Control Guard in Algersiras says (Lieutenant Ramon Cortes Guardia Civil): We realised we couldn't wait until illegal immigrants arrived on the boat. We had to try to stop them as early as possible (Crime Control). If people enter Spanish waters, we are obliged to save them (Social Welfare). What starts as a border control operation (Crime Control), ends up being a Salvage (rescued from dangerous shark infested water and dangerous tides) operation (Social Welfare).

That is what made us think that the operation had to be taken to African waters. This can be seen as another example of surveillance simultaneously watching out for (Social Welfare) and Watching over (Crime Control).

CHAPTER 3

POLICY AND THE SOCIAL SCIENCES AND LITERATURE

POLICY

Crime Control cannot be easily separated from Social Welfare in the Concept of public policies aimed at promoting Security. In response to such pressures of fear of crime, crime, violence and incivilities (anti-social behaviour), Cochrane et al highlight a dual system of public policy in the entanglement between Social Welfare and Crime Control policies. This being firstly "Punitive Segregation" – a Crime Control policy aimed at punishing offenders to bring about justice through e.g. hefty / longer prison sentences, and, secondly, "Preventative Partnership" – a Social Welfare policy which favours working to control crime through community partnership to prevent social problems such as crime and incivility (anti-social behaviour) before they emerge, such as applying 'Situational Crime Prevention' by placing physical barriers such as CCTV between the opportunistic criminal looking for an opportunity to commit crime and the object of crime (Garland 2001a in Cochrane et al, 2008, pP12 - 17).

Both Punitive Segregation and Preventative Partnerships are public policies relating to Restorative Justice (restoring loss suffered by victims of crime by holding offenders accountable for the harm they have caused (Crime Control) and building peace within communities by mobilising communities to take responsibility in safeguarding themselves/their welfare (social welfare) through i.e. CCTV, neighbourhood-watch, Gated Communities (responsibilisation).

In response to Social Policies (Public Policy's dual system of Social Welfare and Crime Control) regarding 'Punitive Segregation' (Crime Control) and 'Preventative Partnership' (Social Welfare approach), people like Felicia's family embrace risk management and situational engineering or situational crime prevention discussed above (Welfare Approach to controlling Crime) by moving into Gated Communities so that Crime or the fear of crime do not impact on their quality of life (Social Welfare).. By moving into Gated Communities, the concern or risk management and situational crime prevention is to reduce risk of crime (risk management) so that they feel safe and secure because of new electronic technologies which monitor or surveill human behaviour (within the walls of the Gated Communities). As Felicia recounts: Despite "some reservations [on the perceived sense of security attached to Gated Communities, nonetheless]...It allows them the freedom to walk around the neighbourhood at night,... safely" (Cochrane et al, 2008, Security, p42) Such new electronic technological surveillance systems place Criminals under the gaze of electronic inspection and every person (entering and leaving) is monitored as a potential surveillance object to deter crime (situational crime prevention). This shows that Crime Control cannot be easily separated from Social Welfare.

++++++++++++++++++++j

Garland (2001) suggests a drift towards punitive segregation by the criminal justice system.

Cochrane et al supports this view. Cochrane et al note that when governments are faced with issues of security (public welfare/safety against crime and fear of crime), government tends to respond by passing more draconian laws and escalating prison rates (harsher prison sentences)

For example, Cochrane et al in Morris (2006) observes for example 3023 new offences were created between 1988 and 1994.

Also Cochrane et al observe data from the International Centre of Prison Studies, 2007. They point out that in England and Wales, prison population significantly increased from 44,719 in 1992 to 80229 in 2007.

Both Criminal Justice Policy and Crime itself tend to bear in often disproportionate ways upon the poorest and most vulnerable in society (in need also of social welfare resources such as Education, job training and mental health and help) – this show entanglement between social welfare and crime control. This is also a social policy issue. For example Cochrane et al report, using research evidence that, the country's growing prison population is characterised by alarming levels of past disadvantage, illiteracy and mental also that (in Wacquant 2001, 2005) in USA "70%" of prison population are (page 14) black or latino (of ethnic minority origin).

Page 13 , page 14 (comment)

Singleton et al 1998 observes, 72% of male sentenced prisoners had two or more mental disorders.

However,

Page 188 in the Journal 'The Myth of Punitiveness' by Roger Matthews (2005), Matthews observes the crime data differently, that there isn't a drift towards punitiveness – e.g. harsher / longer prison sentences, but rather the high prison population is due to new forms of behaviourism (new offences created), monitoring and surveillance technology (e.g. CCTV) together with government policy focused on "what works".

CHAPTER 3

POLICY AND THE SOCIAL SCIENCES AND LITERATURE

POLICY

This concept of community being interpreted in the Policy document is **'place-based'** not 'identity-based' interpretation of Community. This is because 'identity-based' communities suggest that is non-spatial or has infinite locations and is based on what Tonnies terms *"Gesellschaft - urbanised, fragmented and modern society"* linked to shared culture or shared self-interests and weak social ties e.g. no common belonging within a locality which reinforces social ties. (Tönnies, F. (1963) Community and Society, New York, Harper Row in Mooney et al, 2009, Community, p13)

Rather, the concept of community being interpreted in the Policy document embraces what Tonnies's describes as *"Gemeinschaft"* ties which are *"locally based unified and traditional community"* (Tönnies, F. (1963) Community and Society, New York, Harper Row in Mooney et al, 2009, Community, p13). The idea of Gemeinschaft is that close-knit, personal, stable, collective and social relationships are built through *"networks"* of *"trust"* and *"engagement"* or 'interaction' with other residents, local authorities and voluntary and community organisation within a geographical location. (Mooney et al, Community, 2009, pp26 - 27).

For example, drawing from the descriptive summary provided above of Chapters 2 and 3 of the Policy document, 'Gemeinschaft' community ties are being interpreted in Policy initiatives in terms of Governance of local Communities or geographic Communities (communities based on locality). For instance, the Policy document points out that the Community Governance within geographic Communities are much more desired since such local Communities are places where most of the problems are taking place and so *"Community Governance"* works *"close*[r] *to local communities"* than the State and so will be better able to *"solve the problems"* of the local

Community e.g. solving problem populations attached to crime and deprivation and solving problems as places of slum and insecurity towards achieving *"cleaner, safer and greener"* and *"economic growth"* or economic prosperity associated with higher education attainment and higher income levels (Deputy Prime Minister, January 2005, Sustainable Communities: People Places and Prosperity, Chapters 2, p10 and p12). So the community is a site of social policy and governance

Hence, Community Governance combines *"trust"* and networks or *"partnerships"* e.g. Local Strategic Partnerships (LSPs) that *"engage....local people* [mobilised] *to be in lead, business, local government leadership, ...voluntary and community sector.... local police, reformed Fire and Rescue Services* [engagement through the directions of the State / central government]" (Deputy Prime Minister, January 2005, Sustainable Communities: People Places and Prosperity, Chapters 2 and 3, p12, p13, p20, p27). Nonetheless, Community stated within the Policy document is viewed as problem in terms of *"problem populations"* of deprivation and Crime and *"problem places"* of slums and urban decay, and also Community is viewed as a solution to problem populations and problem places through *"Community Governance"*. As Mooney et al observe, that Community Governance is *"local community-based networks" (Mooney et al, 2009, Community, p118)*.

The Policy document also uses research evidence to suggest that some problem populations within some problem places are still *"harder to reach"* and thus lack community that *"nearly two-thirds of children of Pakistani and Bangladeshi descent are growing up in poverty* (Deputy Prime Minister, January 2005, Sustainable Communities: People Places and Prosperity, Chapter 2, p15). Such statistical research evidence could have made use of qualitative personal narrative accounts to suggest why this is. For example, Mooney et al observe that white working class communities combine *"culture / ethnicity and place in an image of belonging* [through being] *natural and historically legitimate occupiers "*. However, Bangladeshi communities are only communities *"based on culture / ethnicity and cannot belong to the locality"* but have the right to social welfare entitlements through citizenship. (Mooney et al, 2009, Community, p89 and p91). Both communities are social heterogeneous (not homogenous) and do not share the same sense of locality and belonging and thus would create tensions around place. Such revelations poses problems for the vision of community interpreted in the Policy document, e.g. community based on social relationships within a locality. 193So certain assumptions are made bout the homogeneity of community

within the complex entanglement between Social Welfare Services and Crime Control measures, Evidence is not used very much to describe how Policy initiatives like New Deal for Communities (NDC) and the various Community Partnerships has improved the quality of well-being / social welfare of citizens in relation to Crime (as a measurement of well-being). The data just says whether local people are happy with NDCs. Here a variety of research evidence of Quantitative data with accompanying Qualitative data (e.g. Case Studies) from a diverse range of Stakeholders involved with the Community Partnership would give a fuller picture to the impact of such Social Welfare policies on the lives of the local community. Example – page 46 – police keen to demostrate taking crime seriously. Page 50 lack of confidence by residents in local CDRP crime control agencies, which helped undermine the attempts of community engagement (social welfare agency).

Page 106 - CDRP /CSP consists of police, police authorities, fire and health along agencies from statutory voluntary sector.

The basis of Community Safety Partnerships (CSP)s is Situational Crime Prevention and Social Crime Prevention by *"reducing opportunities* [of crime by opportunistic criminals] *through situational measures* [e.g. preventative technologies CCTV and alley gates, and also Wardens] near objects of Crime in Community Spaces (Mooney et al, Community, 2009, p105). The idea of (CSP)s is to provide a social welfare approach to Controlling Crime.

Alongside, the basis of Crime and Disorder Reduction Partnership (CDRP) is having *"communitarian-inspired powers"* to deal with social transgression and law breaking. It aims to *"tackle disorder and antisocial behaviour through establishment of exclusion orders, such as Child Curfew and Parenting and Anti-social Behaviour Orders"* or ASBOS (Mooney et al, Community, 2009, p105). Thus CDRP is clearly a punitive- Crime Conrtol approach to safeguarding the quality of life (Social Welfare of residents in the local Community area troubled by Crime (problem place).

....

The Policy initiative that I will describe which I have chosen to identified from Chapters 2 and 3 of the Policy document is the concept of **Social Capital through their idea of 'place-based' Community.**

Mooney et al define Social Capital as *" trust and connectedness between people, and the strong social networks and resources that develop from this ......* [the emphasis here] *on 'people power' and social trust [and networks]"* to create *"and healthier, better educated, [and] more caring communities"* (Mooney et al, Community, 2009, p22, p26 - 27). Additionally, Malcolm Moseley and Ray Pahl in Mooney et al identify Social Capital in three key ways (Bonding Social Capital, Bridging Social Capital and Linking Social Capital). Bonding Social Capital reinforces *"homogenous groups"* or the same groups. Bridging Social Capital bridges *"outward"* relations with *"heterogeneous groups"* (or groups different from each other such as friends and associates) within the community. Finally, Linking Social Capital refers to building relations with *"external sources of power, outside agencies and resources".* (Moseley, M.J. and Pahl, R.E. (2007) Social Capital in Rural Places: A Report to Defra, London, The Stationery Office. In Mooney et al, 2009, Community p139). Thus the type of Social Capital mobilised in the Policy Document are local people *"Bridging Social Capital"* with one and other, and also local people *"linking Social Capital"* by building relations with external sources of power including local authorities, the Police and outside agencies such as the Voluntary and Community Sector and Community based partnerships such as New Deal for Communities (NDC).

Thus the successful engagement of Anne Glover's local Community in the New Deal for Communities programme helped her community build Social Capital based on Bridging Social Capital and Linking Social Capital. This is because Communities without Social Capital are often viewed as deprived communities lacking Community

194

partnerships and experiencing Poverty and such Poor communities or places are often communities where Crime mostly persists. Therefore, this highlights the entanglement between Social Welfare (communities having social capital) and Crime Control (communities with crime control/reduction).

References

Low, S. (2003) Behind the Gates: Life, Security and the Pursuit of Happiness in Fortress America, New York and London, Routledge, in Mooney, G., and Neal, S. (2009) 'Community: Welfare, Crime and Society', England: Open University Press.

Mooney, G., and Neal, S. (2009) 'Community: Welfare, Crime and Society', England: Open University Press.

Moseley, M.J. and Pahl, R.E. (2007) Social Capital in Rural Places: A Report to Defra, London, The Stationery Office, in Mooney, G., and Neal, S. (2009) 'Community: Welfare, Crime and Society', England: Open University Press.

Office of the Deputy Prime Minister (January 2005) Sustainable Communities: People, Places and Prosperity, Office of the Deputy Prime Minister.

(Tönnies, F. (1963) Community and Society, New York, Harper Row, in Mooney, G., and Neal, S. (2009) 'Community: Welfare, Crime and Society', England: Open University Press.

CHAPTER 3

POLICY AND THE SOCIAL SCIENCES AND LITERATURE

POLICY

Assigment title:

'To understand crime, we need to understand relations of power'

To introduce, Crime and Deviance has been conceptualised as a social phenomenon through the labelling of groups whose behaviours/actions come to be seen as undermining the idealised norms and values in a given society (i.e. traditional capitalist, patriarchal, white, Christian way of life in Western Societies). So their behaviours fall in the category of being identified as Crime Problem of Problem People' for Criminal Justice System where such behaviours need to be regulated to prevent Social Harm to society. Also, the behaviours often regulated are those who often reside in communities / localities / globalities (Local/Global) such as urban Segregation / Slums identified as 'problem places' as they are often equated with crime, violence and disorder which are all forms of Social Harms for Society. Thus, to understand Crime, one needs to understand relations of power in society as what behaviours and actions that come to be identified and labelled as crime (criminalised) are socially constructed by those 'Powerful' Elite Groups in Society including, Courts, Corporation's power in Politics, Policy-Makers, Social Institutions such as Schools, the Media, who have powerful influence over the criminal justice process. The Crime labels constructed by Powerful Elite Groups in Society tend to bear itself often disproportionately among certain groups than others, the Crime Labels bear themselves more on those groups who lack Power in society i.e. it bears it self more on those groups categorically and ontologically socially identified as often marginalised, socially excluded (under-class), facing segregation and social restrictions, in other words, those groups facing economic and social disadvantage. Also, since Crime Labelling is a Social Construction because it is relative to or changes with different forms of behaviour, at different times and in different places, in some historical periods and not others. However, firstly I will begin by defining how Crime is a Construction of Law, and also how Crime is Socially Constructed.

Tappan argues Crime is a Construction of Law, that *"Crime is an intentional act in violation of criminal law (statutory and case law), committed without defence or excuse and penalised by the state as a felony or misdemeanour"* (Tappan 1947, p 100 in Muncie et al 2010 , page 4). Additionally Muncie's add that the Crime must show 'criminal intent (mens rea) and voluntary action (actus reus) and 'innocent until proven guilty'. Thus for Tappan Criminal behaviour is any behaviour in violation of the law, and for him this is sufficiently discerning or fair (objective) because the due process of the Criminal Law (it's process) is often full of checks and balances (or filters) as the offenders move through the various stages of the criminal justice process, and these filters may result in a resolution to their case prior to it being full adjudicated within the criminal courts, rather than being punished if no filters were put in place.

Thus for Tappan, the problem of approximation (i.e. accurately identifying) who is a criminal is achieved by asserting that convicted offenders represent the closest possible approximation to those who have violated the criminal law and have come to be identified as criminals through the selective processes of detention, prosecution and punishment. Hence Tappan's definition of Crime as a Construction of Law suggests that it would be morally wrong to identify someone as a criminal unless they had been formally convicted of a crime in accordance with the due process of the law.

As Tappan puts it himself *"'crime' label should be applied only to those acts successfully prosecuted as violations of criminal law"*. Thus, Tappan, asserts that because of this due process of law those offences typically committed by business people are inherently different from criminal offences. (Tappan, 1947 pp96-102 in Muncie et al, 2010, page 148)

However, Crime is also considered as a Social Construct by social actors (Elite Groups) who regulate the behaviours of those identified as problem people through naming, labelling, defining and mapping them into a place because their behaviours come to be seen as social problems or problematic due to the harm their behaviour cause for society, for these elite groups and for their economic, social and political interests. For example, as observed in 01, the use of Opium can be legal and the use of Opium became illegal (Crime) within certain social contexts where the actions of users took place (e.g. if Crimes of the Street were being committed) and the popular reaction 'as a social problem' it received, e.g. from the Media.

Hence for American Sociologist Howard Becker, the causes of crime are not identified in individual behaviours, social factors, social institutions and the quality of the act a person committed. Instead, a deviant or criminal is an offender *"one to whom that* [Crime] *label has been successfully applied"* by others of rules and sanctions. Therefore *"deviant* [or criminal] *behaviour is behaviour that people* [Social Actors/Elite Groups] *label* [as deviant/criminal]*"* (Becker, 1963 p9 in Muncie et al, 2010, p13).

Moreover, in understanding Crime and the Power Relations it has, these social actors (Elite Groups who have economic political and social power to influence the Criminal Justice Process and Policy) are located in Social Institutions, who apply Deviant or Crime Labels to behaviours they define as falling outside defined social norms, values and traditions. For example, although it is usually defined that the conduct of taking the life of another as murder, the Army (often labelled as heroes) and State (commonly thought of as safeguarding the welfare of citizens) provides itself with the legitimate 'Power' to execute (kill) some offenders in the name of Punishment. For example, Muncie et al observe 'The United Nations (UN) Convention against Torture (Social Harm) and Other Cruel Inhuman or Degrading Treatment or Punishment. The UN Convention sees a Criminal offence as *"any act by which severe pain or suffering, whether physical or mental, is intentionally inflicted on a person for such purposes as obtaining from him or a third person information or a confession"* (, 2010, page 218 - 219).

However, the State do not always uphold this UN Convention in their practices, as Muncie et al observe, the State which is commonly understood as associated with the safeguarding of the welfare of citizens, hence commonly understood as a *"'protector'* [against crime] *rather than 'perpetrator of crime'"* provides itself with legitimate 'Power' to Torture prisoners (e.g. of war) which transgresses away from the UN Convention as illustrated in Figure 7.2 (Muncie et al, 2010, page210).   In Figure 7.2, is a photo showing just one of the image testimonies of Torture (a person being identified and labelled as a 'Prisoner' by the US Army (and State) being made to stand on a wooden narrow box wearing a dunce hat with arms stretched wide for balancing support. These testimonies are just one of many Iraqis given Crime Labels 'Prisoners' by US Army and State to justify tortured (punished) by American Soldiers for purpose of interrogation in Abu Ghraib Prison (Muncie et al, 2010, page 218 - 219).

Similarly, in understanding Crime and the relations of Power it has, Sutherland observes that Powerful Business and professional men (corporations), have the economic, political and social power (powerful economic, political and social actors) to influence the implementation of Criminal Law for their own ends in protecting their social norms, values traditions, political, social, and economic interests (e.g. the local/global environmental pollution their business causes in obtaining material wealth).   As Sutherland puts it himself, they have *"the power of their class to influence the implementation and administration of the law"*. (Sutherland, 1983 in Muncie et al, 2010, page 147, and page166)

Thus those defied, labelled, stereotyped as Criminals and represented in Crime Statistics tend to 'inadequately' bear more on the *"criminal behaviour...pathology of the lower-class individuals and their families"* – hence this amounting to social/criminal injustice of certain Categorical Social Identities and Ontological Social Identities (IBID) who are identified and given Crime Labels. Categorical identity relates to the social categories of 'race', gender, age, disability, sexuality, social status etc – Sameness; ontological identity relates to a coherent sense of self – uniqueness.

Similarly, within most Western societies the forms of conduct most likely to be defined as unlawful are those which threaten to undermine the traditional capitalist, patriarchal, white, Christian way of life. For example, it is claimed that the criminal justice system upholds the interests of the Ruling Elite within society by placing a disproportionate amount of its time and effort on policing, prosecuting and punishing 'Crimes Of The Street' , those Social Harms such as assault, robbery, burglary, vandalism and some sexual offences (especially violent offences such as: murder, rape and robbery), which are disproportionately carried out by those "Powerless" socially and economically disadvantaged groups facing social exclusion, deprivation, marginalisation, social restriction and segregation, relative to 'Crimes Of The Suites' committed by Powerful Business Corporations (Corporate Crimes) . For example, in terms of Local/Global Crime, Muncie et al observe that Segregation, Slums, and Mega Slum which are now emerging are problematic places to the norms and values of all societies, whom are often symbolic to poverty and in need of welfare, because they are *"often equated with Crime, Violence and disorder"* (Muncie et al, 2010, page 54). Also, Media exaggeration of Crime and Police Crime Statistics often disproportionately represents these same socially excluded (underclass) in Crime.

For example, Muncie et al identify in Extract 2.1 by Borehamwood and Elstree Times, "[a Police] *gadget* [often used to control pigeons] *which emits a high frequency noise audible only to young people* [under the age of 25]" as the *"latest weapon in the fight against anti-social behaviour in Hertsmere"* (Muncie et al, 2010, page 49). In terms of Local/Global Crime, Hertsmere is a place identified here as problematic (has a crime problem) because it has identified and labelled the youth and their anti-social behaviour as a crime problem people for Hertsmere. Nonetheless, in understanding Crime, the relations of Power it has and it's ability to Socially Construct Crime, this gadget those not distinguish between criminals/deviants and non-criminals/non-deviants, its labelling effect (all youths under the age of 25 can hear it) means that all those youth / young people who are not criminals/deviants will also be punished unjustly (Social Harm) by the Criminal Justice System and Police as they too will be able to pick up the high frequency noise emitted by the gadget. Therefore, this then makes the labelling nature of the gadget Subjectively Problematic to all young people/youth under the age of 25 because it individualises certain categorical and ontological social identities e.g. all young people under 25 years old as a crime problem and this is not an Objective in identifying Crime and Criminals/Deviants.

Similarly, in understanding Crime and the power relations it has, 'Crimes Of The Suites' or 'White Collar Crime' carried out by those Powerful Businesses/Corporations in society, have disparities to 'Crimes of the Street' (often identified as committed by socially excluded marginalised groups) as they tend to be hidden crimes, under-reported crimes and are rarely prosecuted crimes. Those Social Harms caused by 'White Collar Crime' including Fraud, Tax Evasion, Insider Trading, Unlawful Working Practices And Environmental Pollution, tend to be carried out by large, economically Powerful Corporations. Despite Business awareness of Corporate Social Responsibility or CSR to behave responsibly towards society and the environment, and this disparity in 'White Collar Crimes' also occurs despite the fact that the unlawful behaviour of businesses can often result in more Social Harm to society than 'Crimes of the Street'. Muncie et al note the true amount of Corporate Crimes is a 'hidden figure' because Corporate Crimes are handled differently from Civil Crimes because Corporate Crimes *are normally dealt with using different types of authorities ('regulatory') law"* and because of this, Corporate Crimes *"typically remain outside the ambit of mainstream criminal legal procedures"* (Muncie et al, 2010, page 149). For example, Muncie et al highlight that in the case of local/global environmental pollution Crime related to deaths (Social Harm) locally (and globally e.g. in the form of climate change), the term used by Department of Health to describe premature death by pollution are not generally subjected to any process of investigation, partly because of the complexities of investigating and prosecuting such cases, including being able to 'prove living or working' close to *"major source of pollution"*. Hence, in the *"seven years between 2000 and 2007, the Environmental Agency to the UK prosecuted 'only' ninety-nine industrial pollution offences"* (Whyte, EA, 2008 in Muncie et al, 2010, page 150)

Furthermore, the Media has a powerful effect on the fear of Crime and Crime Labelling of Criminals/Deviants. This is unacceptable (is a social/criminal injustice), when so often Media Crime reporting tends to bear itself more on those that are marginalised and often socially excluded in an unbalanced way. The Media often use Exaggeration and Distortion through applying sensational and melodramatic language, labels and stereotyping in Crime and Crime Violence (including rowdiness)

Reporting. Additionally, Media Crime Report often represents 'Crimes of the Street' rather than 'Crimes of the Suite' as more newsworthy in their amplification or heightening of the fear of crime. Also Media Crime Report often uses cultural signifiers or symbols used to identify and label those whose behaviours come to be seen as undermining the norms and values of the society. For instance, 'youths' labelled with 'anti-social behaviour' (deviants) as observed in the Borehamwood & Elstree Times above, and label elderly and particularly women as vulnerable to 'Stranger Danger' (in reflecting a patriarchal society from a feminist perspective). For example through use of categorical and social age identities, i.e. the 'youth' come to be label with 'anti-social behaviours' as well as their clothes, hair styles, scooters / mopeds) all become negatively portrayed, associated with delinquency and disorder, so that the very mention of the word 'youth' reinforces this tone of delinquency, disorder and 'anti-social behaviour'. For example, Stanley Cohen observes that the *"Mods"* were identified as a 'Moral Panic' by the Media, and through this Moral Panic, the 'Mod' becomes symbolic of a certain status, this being the status of the deviant or delinquent (Cohen, 1973, in Muncie et al, 2010, p47 and p237).

Similarly, Muncie et al identify powerful effect the media has in increasing the fear of crime committed by the socially excluded vulnerable females trafficked as sex slaves in their Extract 4.2 from The Guardian Newspaper. The Guardian Newspaper article identified by Muncie et al titled 'Nighre world of suburban sex slaves' use labelling (often shocking labels created to amplify fear) such as 'nighre' , 'suburban' ', sex slaves', 'prostitutes', 'brothels' as a welfare need in regulating of 'women' (as opposed to the men who use and control these) through equating them with this using language such as 'deportation over protection' and 'anti-trafficking campaign to increase deportation'. (, Muncie et al, 2010, page 109).

In Conclusion, in the understanding Crime and the Power relations it has, the Social Construction of Crime Labels (Criminal Law Categories) reflects on certain types of behaviour, defined as criminal in some historical periods and not others, but also reflects how Criminal Law comes to incorporate from only a portion of relatively homogenous behaviour patterns e.g. the norms, values and traditions (patriarchal etc) that are desired for normal society, are used to judge and label the deviant and criminal behaviours that fall outside the values of Normal Society, and the remainder of other behavioural patterns often heterogeneous, are often excluded, even though each and every instance of this behaviour causes avoidable harm, injury , or deprivation. Rather than being a fair reflection of these behaviours objectively in Criminal Law causing collectively the most avoidable suffering, Criminal Law Categories are social constructs designed to criminalise only some victimising behaviours (subjectively individualising and excluding certain behaviours considered as the wrong way to behave), usually those more frequently committed by the relatively Powerless, and to exclude others, usually those frequently committed by the Powerful (those social control agents including police, law courts as part of the Criminal Justice System/Process, Media and Elite Groups and Businesses in society) against subordinates. In summation, in terms of the Understanding Power Relations of Crime, in criminal justice policy and practice, it is difficult to prove criminals possess biological, psychological or social characteristics not typically found among the law-abiding population. However, the Social Construction of Crime suggest that it is the powerless who are often socially excluded, marginalised and deprived who more often bear the weight of being identified, stereotyped and labelled as deviants/criminals and more often represented in the Media Portrayal of Crime Violence and Police Crime Statistics than other Categorical and Ontological Social Identities. Also, in Understanding the Power Relations of Crime, the Social Construction of Crime suggest that it is the moral values, economic, political and social interests of those Powerful Elites in Society that are upheld in Criminal Law.

References

Assignment Booklet 1, (October 2009J), The Open University

Becker, H. (1963) Outsiders: Studies in the Sociology of Deviance, New York, Free Press **in** Muncie, J., Talbot, D., Muncie, R., (First Edition) (2010) *Crime: Local and Global*, Open University Press/Milton Keynes, The Open University.

Cohen, S. (1973) Folk Devils and Moral Panics: The Creation of Mods and Rockers, St Albans, Paladin, **in** Muncie, J., Talbot, D., Muncie, R., (First Edition) (2010) *Crime: Local and Global*, Open University Press/Milton Keynes, The Open University

Muncie, J., Talbot, D., Muncie, R., (First Edition) (2010) *Crime: Local and Global*, Open University Press/Milton Keynes, The Open University.

Personal communication between David Whyte and Environmental Agency, 4 April 2008 **in** Muncie, J., Talbot, D., Muncie, R., (First Edition) (2010) *Crime: Local and Global*, Open University Press/Milton Keynes, The Open University

Sutherland, E. (1983) White Collar Crime: The Uncut Version, New Haven, CT, Yale University Press **in** Muncie, J., Talbot, D., Muncie, R., (First Edition) (2010) *Crime: Local and Global*, Open University Press/Milton Keynes, The Open University

Tappan, P.R. (1947) 'Who is the criminal?', American Sociological Review, vol.12, no.1, pp.96-102 **in** Muncie, J., Talbot, D., Muncie, R., (First Edition) (2010) *Crime: Local and Global*, Open University Press/Milton Keynes, The Open University

Articles:

'Nighre world of suburban sex slaves' The Guardian, (8 May 2006) <u>in</u> Muncie, J., Talbot, D., Muncie, R., (First Edition) (2010) *Crime: Local and Global*, Open University Press/Milton Keynes, The Open University

'We are not Pigeons' Borehamwood & Elstree Times, (9 March 2006) <u>in</u> Muncie, J., Talbot, D., Muncie, R., (First Edition) (2010) *Crime: Local and Global*, Open University Press/Milton Keynes, The Open University.

CHAPTER 3

POLICY AND THE SOCIAL SCIENCES AND LITERATURE

ENGLISH LITERATURE

The idea of reading and studying the 'classics' of Literature

English Literature is an alternative to ' television culture' . It focuses on aspects of English culture.

Great Expectations by Charles Dickens, theme of Great Expectations suggests wanting to escape and better one self is a universal goal shared by others if not everyone.

Macbeth by William Shakespeare:

GENRE : Genre means style of literature for theatre, radio, or television. For instance Macbeth is defined as a Drama type Genre because it is written in a prose or verse composition, secondly it tells a story that is intended on representation by actors.

LANGUAGE :Using quotations 'I'll fight till from my bones my flesh be hack'd' suggests that Macbeth was not afraid to die

DRAMATIC EFFECT : There were few props or scenery in the early Globe Theatre where William Shakespeare openly acted his plays, but he was able to create reality in the theatre. For example, Macbeth's hallucinations - Macbeth thinks he sees a dagger or sees Banquo's ghost at the banquet. These might be shown using lighting and shadow techniques or in modern day visions (perhaps using a projector), but most audiences now and in Shakespeare's day could have imagined it since the language used is detailed and graphic.

CONTEXT : Context is defined as the circumstances that form the setting for an event, statement, or idea. Macbeth was written 400 years ago by William Shakespeare who was born in Stratford up Avon in 1564. It is suggested that his life and social circumstance was behind the circumstances of Shakespeare writing the play Macbeth. For instance he draws on writing skills from education, probably educated at a grammar school. Shakespeare was married at 18 to wife Anne Hathaway who was eight years older. They had two girls and a boy (who died aged 11). Hence Shakespeare used his life experience to draw on experiences in his play and social settings and periods, e.g. lavish banquets, historical castle buildings, daggers, swords, and candles / non electric lighting, no television suggesting the reason why Shakespeare wrote theatre (drama plays). For example, it is said

'Shakespeare became a leading member of the theatre troupe known as 'The Lord Chamberlain's Men'. The company proved very popular and later, when King James I granted them the right to perform at his court, the troupe became known as 'The King's Men'. Shakespeare wrote over 30 plays for 'The King's Men', making it the most important theatre company in the country, and he often wrote parts for particular actors. He was very successful and wealthy in his time, and his work has remained very popular ever since'.

PLOT : means what the story is about

A Brief plot, the play opens as three witches plan a meeting with the Scottish nobleman Macbeth, at the moment of a great battle, who forecast of things to come for Macbeth, who takes it literally and ensure he attains the prophecy even not being afraid to kill his friends, not even afraid to die, draws on his skills as a soldier.

CHARACTER : character means the nature of a person, the mental and moral qualities distinctive to an individual. We know that Macbeth is a brave and valiant soldier, ready to die for his king, Duncan, because he is a soldier and took a soldier's oath to die for king and country, normal route of a soldier is through oath of allegiance. However, the prophecies of the witches have a powerful effect on him, especially when he learns the first has come true, and he becomes the Thane of Cawdor. He thinks more and more about being king, and he is easily persuaded to agree to murder Duncan. However, he often appears weak - he starts to have visions, he asks lots of questions, he cannot make a decision and never really seems sure of himself. For instance, he panics just after the murder and has to rely on his wife to find an alibi.

THEMES : the theme is the subject setting or ambience of the piece of writing or play, Macbeths reaction towards the witches prophecies and the outcome of his reaction when he kills his friends, such an outcome of good conquers over evil, a universal idea that his shared. For instance the witches are traditionally lack integrity and worthiness which leads on to Macbeth about issues of trusting what other say based on their position e.g. witches seen as alternative wisdom, and Macbeths fall at the end all suggest good conquers over evil.

CHAPTER 3

POLICY AND THE SOCIAL SCIENCES AND LITERATURE

PARETO EFFIECIENCY AND COMPETITIVE EQUILIBRIUM

EFFICIENCY AND EQUILIBRIUM

IMPROVING EFFICIENCY - WELFARE THEOREM , WELFARE POLICIES, DISTRIBUTIONAL POLICIES

The notion that a competitive equilibrium promotes economic well-being is based on the argument that a competitive equilibrium is Pareto Efficient. In that it is impossible to improve any agents situation (e.g. Person A or Person B in an equilibrium/situation without someone else worse off. Best Pareto Efficiency is C where Person A has the same balance or value as
Person B.

Person A
... .
  .   .
  .   .
  .   .
  .   .
  .   .C
  .   .
  .   .
     .
   .
.... Person B

CHAPTER 3

POLICY AND THE SOCIAL SCIENCES AND LITERATURE

ASSYMETRIC INFORMATION AND HOW YOU SORT 'LEMON' CAR INFORMATION, STARTING POINT ALL SECOND HAND CARS ARE LEMON CARS NO WAY OF TELLING CAR WORKS UNLESS TAKE IT HOME AND TEST IT OUT

asymmetric information when all relevant information is known to one party and not the other information is generally incomplete this is known as a 'lemons' problem just as in the 'prisoners dilemma' where the prisoner has to collaborate his story with that of his assailant in the pay-off matrix, in the lemons situation there is no transparent way of telling the advertised sale of a car is a lemon or incomplete car unless buy it take home and try it, the idea of the lemons situation is that decision making between two parties buyer and seller should have enough information to solve the market problem, so despite buyers limits on cost and effort screening transparency such as 'adverse selection' ensures or the sale transaction information of the cars are all on similar terms, they are lemons but no party is worse of because all transaction information on the cars are the same. 'moral hazard' occurs when one party to a contract can take advantage of asymmetric information/incomplete information

CHAPTER 3

POLICY AND THE SOCIAL SCIENCES AND LITERATURE

Project task: Write an extended essay on the project of your choice

Topic Title: Determinants of Wage Biases in the UK Labour Market

CONTENTS PAGE

Project task: Write an extended essay on the project of your choice

Topic Title: Determinants of Wage Biases in the UK Labour Market

1 - INTRODUCTION:

For the Purposes of the Quantitative Analysis Project regarding Wage Discrimination and Wage Differentials, during my period at Residential School at the University of Bath, I obtained a set of Econometric Results. Econometrics is the application of statistics to study economic data, in this case Wage Discrimination and Wage Differentials. The Econometric Results was obtained using Dummy Variables (where Dummy Variables in a regression model have two categories, valued zero and 1, where e.g. male = 0 and female = 1). The

211

Econometric Results is also based on the Ordinary Least Square (OLS) Linear Regression which is a technique used for estimating the unknown parameters (relationship between e.g. dependent γ Variable Wages and independent χ Variable Region etc) in a linear regression model by employing formals such as adjusted R squared (R^2) and P-Value etc. My Econometric Results uses Multiple Regression (defined below) for the basis of looking at number of casual factors (independent χ Variables) such as Employment, being Female etc., to test for any relationship with the dependent γ Variable Wages, in order to find any evidence to support the Alternative Hypothesis of Wage Differentials or in the extreme case, if the strength of relationship is strong enough between the dependent γ Variable, and multiple χ Variables, suggesting evidence for the Null Hypothesis that Wage Discrimination may exist.

Wage differentials (gaps between different wages have both economic explanations e.g. if one worker produces more (economic) output than another, and non-economic explanations e.g. if one worker works longer hours than another, and also the type of profession both workers are engaged in. However, Wage discrimination occurs when workers' wages for the same job differs between them for reasons that are unrelated to the value of the (economic) output of the worker, e.g. due to gender such as being Female, age, ethnicity or living in a particular Region.

Understanding that there will be Wage Differentials attributed to casual factors such as Work Output which when increased, also increases higher pay, however, I would like to use my Econometric Results obtained using Dummy Variables to investigate whether there is evidence to support the Null Hypothesis that there Wage Discrimination i.e. being paid lower wages based living in a particular Region and being Female, which are unrelated to economic output or human capital of the worker (human capital being, as human capital increases, Wages also increases). Thus, my objective in this project is to test the Null Hypothesis (Ho) in order to find out whether there is evidence to support the Null Hypothesis of Wage Discrimination in Labour Market. If no Wage Discrimination persists, using supporting formulas such as using the Significance levels as guide to determine the rejection region, I will then reject the Null Hypothesis, in favour of the Alternative Hypothesis (H_1 or Ha) that different levels of Wages are explained by Wage Differentials in Human Capital.

With regards to Key Sources and Resources, My Econometric Results makes use of Open University Data Set (Dummy Variables) which are Analysed in MS Excel using OLS Regression Analyses (define above) and Interpreted using Econometric formulas including Adjusted R Squared (R^2), P- Value etc as discussed below. I will also support the validity of my Quantitative Statistical Econometric Results Analyses with a variety of Qualitative Secondary/Existing Research Evidence. The Qualitative Secondary Research Evidence I will be referring to are Becker's Model of Employer's Taste and Mincer on Human Capital.

Nevertheless, in relation, the term **Correlation** implies that both the Dependent γ (Y) Variable WAGES and the Independent χ (X) Variables have some sort of linear relationship which I will investigate by analysing Dummy Variables into Multiple Regression and Interpret using Mean Average formulas such as Adjusted R Squared and P-Value to name a few. Similarly, the term Causation implies a change in the Independent X Variables will cause a change in the Dependent y variable WAGES to happen. I will prove the strength of the Causation using Mean Average formulas such as P-Value and Confidence Level obtained from performing a Multiple Regression Analyses on Dummy Variable data sets.

2 – HYPOTHESIS TESTING

Hypothesis Testing is statistical procedure in the form of statistical inference that uses data (e.g. Dummy Variables) to test and existing claim about the population. This claim about the population is denoted by Ho (which is the Null Hypothesis). If the data supports the claim it is to accept the Null Hypothesis (Ho). However, generally, a Hypothesis Test is designed to show that the existing claim on the population is false, so to reject the Null Hypothesis (Ho) in favour of concluding an Alternative Hypothesis (Ha / H_1).

Hypothesis Test is set up using the Null Hypothesis as the result that is believed before the study. My Null Hypothesis is to investigate whether there is there is Wage Discrimination unrelated to the worker's Economic Output produced (or Number of Hours worked) or Human Capital (skills, experience) but rather related to the worker living in a certain Region or being Female

Since the Hypothesis Test is based on sample size information about population and not the true population size, the possibility of errors must therefore be considered, using e.g. Margin of Error (Confidence Interval), Confidence Level, and Significance level, P-Value, critical value etc discussed below.

But first, the Null Hypothesis (Ho) could be defined as the current situation which everyone assumes was true before my analyses test. The Alternative Hypothesis (Ha) represents the Alternative Hypothesis Model (H_1/Ha) that I want to consider and prove with my hypothesis research test.

Hence, Linear Regression particularly Multiple Regression allows the Researcher to test the validity of the Null Hypothesis.

3 – LINEAR REGRESSION, SIMPLE REGRESSION, MULTIPLE REGRESSION:

Simple Linear Regression is a technique used to determine a straight line that best fits a data.

The equation for a straight line, known as a linear equation takes the form: $\hat{y} = a + bx$

Where:

$\hat{y}$ = (y hat which is) the predicted value of y , give the value of χ (y is predicted value because it is not the true population size but a sample size)

χ = the independent variable

a = y-intercept for the straight line which is the Intersection with the y axis, in other words it is the point at which the point at which the line crosses the y-axis.

b = the slope / gradient of the straight line, which is the ratio of the rise of the line over the run of the line. Thus a positive slope indicates that the line is rising from left to right, while a negative slope moves lower from left to right. If b = 0, the line is horizontal, which means there is no relationship between the independent χ Variable and dependent variable, in other words that, a change in the value of x has no effect on the value of y.

However, Simple Linear regression is limited to examining the relationship between the dependent variable (γ Variable), and only one independent variable (χ Variable). Hence Multiple Regression allows for more than one independent variable (γ Variable) in the relationship with the dependent variable (γ Variable). Thus the Multiple Regression equation formula for this Multiple Regression method is :

$\hat{y} = a + b_1\chi_1 + b_2\chi_2 + ...+b_n\chi_n$, or

$\gamma = a + b_1\chi_1 + b_2\chi_2 + e$, or

$\gamma = \alpha + \beta_1 x_1 + \beta_2 x_2 + \varepsilon$

$\gamma = a + b_1\chi_1 + b_2\chi_2 + e$, in other words $\gamma = \alpha + \beta_1 x_1 + \beta_2 x_2 + \varepsilon$

Where y is the dependent variable

x_1 is the first independent variable

x_2 is the second independent variable ,

α and β are parameters of the model where in the linear term of $\alpha + \beta_1 x_1 + \beta_2 x_2$ is the **variations in y that can be explained by** x.

ε is the error of prediction (also known as random variable, error term, outlier, or residual) and is also a random variable, where $e = y - \hat{y}$. e is the error in using $\hat{y}$ to estimate y.

The error term of ε *is* variations in γ *Variable* that **can not be explained** by the **linear relationship** between χ *Variable* and γ *Variable.*

When the regression line is linear (y = ax + b) the Regression Coefficients are the Y intercept or Constant (a), the x and γ Variables, and the slope of the regression line that represents the rate of change of one variable (y) as a function of changes in the other variable (x).

Hence, of which the objective of OLS regression is to obtain a regression coefficient and an intercept that minimises the sum of the Squared Errors (outliers). Thus Error of Prediction is important as it takes into account the squared errors (outliers) and tells the Researcher how well the model fits the data, in other words, it Ordinary Least Square Regression line yields the best prediction of the (average) Dependent Y Variable WAGES for any value of Independent X Variables one might choose to use.

The Dummy Variables that I have chosen to test are to prove the validity of the Null Hypothesis that there is Wage Discrimination unrelated to the worker's Economic Output (Work Hours) or Human Capital (skills, experience) but rather related to the worker living in a certain Region or being Female.

I will employ the Multiple Linear Regression Equation into my Analyses

$$y = \alpha + \beta_1 x_1 + \beta_2 x_2 + \beta_3 x_3 + \beta_4 x_4 + \beta_5 x_5 + \beta_6 x_6 + \beta_7 x_7 + \varepsilon \ , \quad \text{where:}$$

y represents WAGES

x_1 represents FEMALE

x_2 represents ALEVEL & DEGREE

x_3 represents PROFESSIONAL & MANAGERIAL

x_4 represents ENGINEER

x_5 represents GREATER LONDON

x_6 represents AGE

x_7 represents EXPERIENCE, which is obtained by squaring the Dummy Variables for AGE.

Therefore, Multiple Regression equation represents:

WAGES = $\beta0$ + $\beta1$ *(FEMALE)* + $\beta2$ *(ALEVEL & DEGREE)* + $\beta3$ *(PROFESSIONAL& MANAGERIAL)* + $\beta4$ *(ENGINEER)* + $\beta5$ *(GREATER LONDON)* + $\beta6$ *(AGE)* + $\beta7$ *(EXPERIENCE)* + ε

Where,

FEMALE Coefficient shows that on average females earn £12,000 less than men

ALEVEL + DEGREE Coefficient shows that on average if one has an Alevel + Degree you earn £9,000 more

PROFESSIONAL & MANAGERIAL Coefficient shows that on average if one has Professional or Managerial qualifications they earn £16,000 more

ENGINEERING Coefficient shows that on average if one is employed as an Engineer they earn £188 more which is not a lot.

GREATER LONDON Coefficient show that on average if one is working in Greater London, then they are likely to earn on average almost £7,000 more

AGE Coefficient shows that with age (as one gets older) they are likely to earn almost £2,000 more

EXPERIENCE Coefficient shows that with experience (as more experience are acquired) income falls by £21

I chose to test these dummy Independent χ variables, because I want to test whether these dummy Independent χ variables (which are casual factors because they are unrelated to Economic Output) could influence or could be strongly associated to the Dependent γ Variable WAGES for one to Accept the Null Hypothesis that **there is Wage Discrimination unrelated to the worker's Economic Output produced (or Number of Hours worked) or Human Capital (Skills and Experience) but rather related to the worker living in a certain Region (Greater London) or being Female**

4 - CONFIDENCE LEVEL, CONFIDENCE INTERVAL, SIGNFICANCE LEVEL (CRITICAL VALUE), P-VALUE:

The Confidence Level is a test which represents how often the same results from the true percentage of the population would be achieved if repeated again and again. Thus a 95% Confidence Level as shown in Table (1) Appendix 1 means that there is 95% certainty that the same results of the Multiple Regression Analyses on the Dummy Variables would be achieved with a repeated sampling (when the test is repeated again and again).

Thus, with a larger sample size of the population rather than a smaller sample size which is further away from the population size, the same results from sample size would be achieved if repeated again and again, thereby increasing the Confidence Level and reducing the Margin of Error, providing there are no bias and the data is collected properly, including prohibiting data fishing (redoing the analyses/test in different ways to get desired results).

The Confidence Interval is also known as the Margin of Error or Error Rate. The Confidence Interval or Margin of Error measures how close the sample result should be to the population parameter (population mean) being studied.

The Confidence Interval or Margin of Error is a complement to the Significance Level (α). Hence a 95% Confidence Interval means a 5% **Significance Level** (at which Confidence Interval = 1 - α, which is basically 100 - α).

The Significance Level (α) which is also the Critical Value gives the maximum allowable probability of making a Type I error – the Significance Level value of which is decided upon before the data sample is collected and analysed, as a guide to avoid or control making a Type I error. Type I Error occurs when the Null Hypothesis (Ho) is not accepted when in reality the Null Hypothesis is true. A Type II Error (β) however, occurs when one fails to reject the Null Hypothesis when in reality, the Null Hypothesis (Ho) is not true.

To avoid making a Type I Error (α) and Type II Error (β), the values of both (α) and (β) need to be as small as possible. If the sample size is relatively small, reducing the value of (α) will result in an increase in the value of (β) – the opposite also holds true. Both (α) and (β) will reduce simultaneously, both at 0 values, once the size of the data sample has been increase to the size of the population. Increasing the sample size has more of a certainty that the Mean truly reflects the Population. However, increasing the sample size to the size of the population in order to reduce (α) and (β) simultaneously is unrealistic for small scale research due to cost, time and one-man power, unless if carried out by Government Household Survey every ten years which has larger funding and more man power..

Likewise, the P-Value measures the likelihood of getting the sample results if the Null Hypothesis were true, and could be defined as the smallest level of significance (observed level of significance) at which the Null Hypothesis will be rejected, assuming the Null Hypothesis (Ho) is true. In most cases, the research attempt is to find support for the Alternative Hypothesis (Ha or H_1). Thus, the smaller the P-Value, the more the (the father out the Test-Statistics is on the Standard Normal Distribution Diagram, and the more confident the researcher can be about rejecting the Null Hypothesis (Ho) in support for the Alternative Hypothesis (H_1 / Ha).

Similarly if the P-Value is less than the **Critical Values (Significance Level)** of 1% (0.01), 5% (0.05), and 10% (0.10) given in Table (1) in the Appendix, means the Null Hypothesis (Ho) that there is Wage Discrimination is not reflective of the population or equal to the Mean of the Population (data sample of Sample Mean distribution of the Population denoted by μ) which confirms that the Researcher Rejects the Null Hypothesis (Ho) and Accepts the (Alternative Hypothesis).

The Critical Value of 1% (0.01), 5% (0.05), and 10% (0.10) which is also the Significance Level (α) gives the maximum allowable probability of making a

Type I error – the Significance Level value of which is decided upon before the data sample is collected and analysed, as a guide to avoid or control making a Type I error.

The Multiple Linear Regression Analyses I obtained from the Dummy Variables has a P-Value of 0.008633147, which is less that the Critical Values (Significance Levels) which the Critical Value gives the maximum allowable probability of making a Type I error – the Significance Level value of which is decided upon before the data sample is collected and analysed, as a guide to avoid or control making a Type I error, as given in Table (1) in the Appendix. Thus, since the P-Value is less that the Critical Values, this provide confidence that we can reject the Null Hypothesis without making a Type I error when the Null Hypothesis (Ho) is not accepted when in reality the Null Hypothesis is true.

5 – R SQUARED OR R^2 (ALSO KNOWN AS COEFFICIENT OF DETERMINATION), ADJUSTED R SQUARED (R^2):

The value of R Squared or R^2 (also known as Coefficient of Determination) measures the percentage of the variability in the Response Variable (γ) explained by the Explanatory Variables (χ) or Regression Line, by looking at the data around the Regression Line in a Linear Equation. Moreover, R-squared measures the variation of the residual values or outliers (also known as random variable or error term) around the regression 'linear' line relative to the overall variation of the data, so that the smaller the variation of residual values shows an R-squared closer to 1.0 which means a strong positive relationship between χ variables White Males and White Females and γ variable wages.

Thus a high value of R-Squared (R^2) closer to 1.0 (100%) at 0.9 or 90% shows that 10% (1.0 – 0.9) of the residual variance is not accounted for by the regression line and 10% being a smaller residual value (outlier) than that the R squared variance indicates that the Regression Line model (defined above of which to test the true validity of the Null Hypothesis) fits the data very well so that there is a strong positive relationship between γ Variable WAGES and χ Variables.

However, in the case of Multiple Regression, the value of Adjusted R^2 is the preferred measured, because it takes R^2 and adjusts it for the number of χ Variables in the Multiple Linear Regression model.

The Multiple Linear Regression Analyses I obtained from the Dummy Variables has a Coefficient of Determination or R squared closer to 0 at 0.23 or 23%. Similarly, the Multiple Linear Regression Analyses I obtained from the Dummy Variables has an Adjusted R Squared (Adjusted $\mathbf{R^2}$) which is also at 0.23 (to 2 decimal places). The R Squared ($\mathbf{R^2}$) variance value of 0.23 (to 2 decimal places) and Adjusted R Squared (Adjusted $\mathbf{R^2}$) variance value of 0.23 (to 2 decimal places) both indicate that about 77% (1-0.23) of the residual variance or outliers is not accounted for by the regression line and 77% being larger than the R squared variance indicates that the regression does not fit the data at all so that there is a very weak relationship between Dependent γ Variable WAGES and the Collective Effect of the Independent χ Variables. For example, both the R Squared ($\mathbf{R^2}$) and Adjusted R Squared (Adjusted $\mathbf{R^2}$) is too weak to suggest that the γ Variables WAGES are accounted for or explained by Collective Effect of the χ Variables and also too weak to the support the Null Hypothesis that there is a Wage Discrimination (when workers' wages for the same job differs between them for reasons that are unrelated to the value of the (economic) output of the worker) based on e.g. Region, being Female). Rather, the R Squared ($\mathbf{R^2}$) and Adjusted R Squared (Adjusted $\mathbf{R^2}$) results suggests that there are Wage Differentials (gaps between different wages) due to economic explanations e.g. if one worker produces more (economic) output than another, and non-economic explanations e.g. if one worker works longer hours than another, and also the type of profession both workers are engaged in.

6 – T-STATISTIC, (ALSO KNOWN AS TEST-STATISTIC):

T-statistic, (also known as Test-Statistic) can be taken from the Student's T-Distribution Table. T-Statistic measures how extreme a statistical estimate is a hypothesised value is reasonable when the T-Statistic is close to 0, or if the T-Statistic is large positive, the hypothesised value is too small which means one should reject Null Hypothesis (Ho) of wage discrimination in favour of Alternative Hypothesis (H_1 / Ha). Similarly if the T-Statistic is large negative then the hypothesised value is too large, which also means one should reject Null Hypothesis (Ho) of wage discrimination in favour of Alternative Hypothesis (H_1 / Ha). For example, The Multiple Linear Regression Result Analyses I obtained from the Dummy Variables has a T-Statistic of -2.63 (to 2 decimal places) showing that there is somewhat not enough evidence to suggest the Null Hypothesis is true that there is Wage Discrimination unrelated to Economic Output or Human Capital.

7 – MULTIPLE R (MULTIPLE CORRELATION COEFFICIENT R):

Nonetheless, Multiple Correlation Coefficient R is what is called Multiple R in a Multiple Regression analysed in MS Excel (the statistical package I used to Regress (analyse) the Dummy Variables. Multiple Linear Regression Result Analyses I obtained from the Dummy Variables includes the Multiple Correlation Coefficient R (Multiple R) or Beta – the slope or gradient in a linear equation. The Coefficient is the degree of strength to which the Predictors / Independent (χ) Variables **have a relationship** to the Independent (γ) variable WAGES. In Multiple Regression, the Multiple Correlation Coefficient R assumes values between 0 and 1 where 0 means the Collective Independent χ Variables have no relationship with the Dependent γ variable WAGES, where 1 means the Collective Independent χ Variables have a relationship with Dependent γ Variables. Also the direction of the relationship between the Independent χ Variables and Dependent γ Variable WAGES is interpreted by looking at whether the value of the Multiple

Correlation Coefficient R is plus or minus so that a negative sign implies a downward sloping or negative relationship between x variables and y variable and a positive sign implies upward sloping or positive relationship.

For example Multiple Linear Regression Result Analyses I obtained from the Dummy Variables has a Multiple Correlation Coefficient R (Multiple R) value of 0.481153 showing a weak positive relation between the Collective Independent χ Variables and Dependent γ Variable WAGES. This weak relationship between the Independent χ Variables and Dependent γ Variable WAGES implies that there is not enough evidence to support the Null Hypothesis, that the Null Hypothesis is the true picture of the population sample.

8 – ECONOMIC THEORIES OF BECKER'S EMPLOYER TASTE ON WAGE DISCRIMINATION RELATING TO NULL HYPOTHESIS (Ho) CHALLENGED BY MY MULTIPLE REGRESSION ANALYSES RESULTS, AND MINCER'S HUMAN CAPITAL SUPPORTED BY MY MULTIPLE REGRESSION ANALYSES RESULTS IN FAVOUR OF ALTRNATIVE HYPOTHESIS (Ha or H₁):

Thus, my Multiple Linear Regression Result Analyses to test the validity of the Null Hypothesis (that there is Wage Discrimination unrelated to Economic Output and Human Capital such as being Female) does not support the Null Hypothesis and there does Becker's (1971) model explanation of Wage Discrimination. **Becker's 'Employer Taste' Neoclassical standard utility maximising model** explanation is based on the idea that "employer's have taste or preference against people from disadvantaged groups such as women or ethnic minorities" (prejudice for unknown reasons) in the same way economist would analyse individual preference between goods and services. Becker (1971) argues that employers or customers do not want to work with or come in contact with worker's who of other racial groups or workers that are women, even though that these workers from disadvantaged groups may be as productive as other workers or be more

224

productive than other workers on which case employer's reduce the employer's profitability. Becker's theory also goes further to suggest that employer's *"would only [maximise their utility by] employ[ing] these disadvantage groups if these workers are paid lower wages"* than the norm – the normal level of wages paid to workers in general, and by doing so employers would increase their 'profitability' (Wells et al, Markets (1988), p81).

Rather, however, my Multiple Linear Regression Result Analyses accepts the Alternative Hypothesis (Ha / H_1), that the formula results of the Multiple Linear Regression are to weak to conclude a Null Hypothesis of Wage Discrimination such as being Female or living in the Greater London Region, and takes into account the less significant variations in WAGES could be explained by Wage Differentials in Economic (Production) Output or Human Capital – less significant WAGE Variation on γ-axis is **explained by the Explanatory Independent Variables (χ) or Regression Line**. For example, Mincer's Human Capital model regarding gender specific roles between males and females or Statistical discrimination model explains this. For Mincer, Human Capital based on the traditional division of labour in the family observe that women earn less and tend to be located in different occupations to men based on the voluntary decision of men and women. For example, Mincer suggest that the longer hours women spend on housework and career breaks due to child-rearing lowers the effort they put into their market jobs compared to men's and hence results in reduced wages for women **(Wells et al, (2002) Households, p148)**. **Statistical discrimination model** is based on human capital theory and argues workers are treated by their employers on the basis of knowledge of the worker's length of time in their investment in education and training (human capital), and workers productivity difference to other workers which both level of investment and productivity can increase income resources.

Statistical discrimination model observes that in terms of productivity, Women have different *"productivity"* (are skilled at different work) to that or Men and so this is reflected in the wage differentials between Women and Men (Wells et al, Markets (2008, p83-84).

Also in terms of Human capital or investment in education and training, the **Statistical Discrimination model** argues women expect to drop out of the labour market because of family responsibilities like child rearing and as result would have undertaken less education and training when they re-enter the labour market. Hence Women will opt for occupations such as nursing, clerical and secretarial in which *"breaks"* from work (due to child rearing) *"incur the smallest penalty"* (Wells et al, Markets (2008, p82).

9 STRENGTHS AND WEAKENESS OF MULTIPLE REGRESSION ANALYSES:

The strengths of my Multiple Regression Analyses Results was that the MS Excel Package gave a lot of Mean Average formulas including Adjusted R Squared, Multiple R and P-Value (to name a few) in which, I was able to use this Averages of the Sample Population Size of 3385 of the Dummy Variables to test the validity of the Null Hypothesis (Ho) of Wage Discrimination unrelated to Economic Production Output and Human Capital (within the Sample Population Size of 3385). Other strengths of my Multiple Regression Analyses Results my ability to Analyse the Dummy Variables data set using Multiple Regression Analysis and, and make correct Interpretations of the Mean Average formulas such as P-Value, Adjusted R Squared etc of which these provided me with enough evidence to reject the Null Hypothesis (Ho) of Wage Discrimination and accept the Alternative Hypothesis (Ha or H_1) of Wage Differentials.

However, a weakness I observed which is not a direct weakness on the results obtained from my Multiple Regression Analyses was that due to time constraints, I was not able to develop my Project through employing 'Interaction Effects' to look at the combined effect of being Female and Industry Type (Female * Industry Type) to finding out whether being Female can affects Women's pay within a particular Industry.

10 – REFERENCES AND KEY SOURCES AND RESOURCES

REFERENCES:

1. Assignment Booklet 1, D319, (2009), The Open University

2. Himmelweit, S., Trigg, A., Costello, N., Dawson, G., Mackintosh, M., Simonetti, R., Wells, J. (2002) *'Households'* Glasgow, The Open University, Bath Press

3. Simonetti, R., Mackintosh, M., Costello, N., Dawson, G., Himmelweit, S., Trigg, A., Wells, J. (2003) *'Firms'* Glasgow, The Open University, Bath Press

4. Trigg, A., Himmelweit, S., Costello, N., Dawson, G., Mackintosh, M., Simonetti, R., Wells, J (2008) 'Markets' Glasgow, The Open University, Bath Press

KEY SOURCES AND RESOURCES:

- Open University Data Set (Dummy Variables)

- MS Excel Statistical Computer Package used to Analyse Dummy Variables in order to produce Ordinary Least Square Regression Analyses

APPENDIX 1 – TABLE OF RESULTS

TABLE OF RESULTS

TABLE (1) showing Multiple Regression Results from Regression Analyses that is Interpreted above in the main body of the Project Report to test the true validity of the Null Hypothesis

SAMPLE SIZE, n (Sample Size of Population Number)	3385
R squared (R^2)	0.231508
Adjusted R squared (Adjusted R^2)	0.229915
Multiple R (Multiple Correlation Coefficient R also known as Multiple R which is the name used in MS Excel Multiple Regression)	0.481153
y – Intercept	-14421.5
P-Value	0.008633147
T-Stat / Test Statistics	-2.62779
χ_1 (FEMALE) Coefficient	-12345.6
χ_2 (ALEVEL & DEGREE) Coefficient	9233.666
χ_3 (PROFESSIONAL & MANAGERIAL) Coefficient	16378.64
χ_4 (ENGINEER) Coefficient	188.9131
χ_5 (GREATER LONDON REGION LOCATION) Coefficient	6798.936
χ_6 (AGE) Coefficient	1914.79
χ_7 (EXPERIENCE) Coefficient = AGE*AGE (obtained by squaring Age)	-21.8775
Significance Levels, also known as Critical Values relating to P-Values are set as: 1% (0.01), 5% (0.05), and, 10% (0.10)	

Multiple Regression Equation Analyses obtained from the Regression of a Selected Dummy Variables used to test the Validity of the Null Hypothesis (Ho) is given below:

$$\gamma = -14421.5 + -12345.6\ \chi_1 + 9233.666\ \chi_2 + 16378.64\ \chi_3 + 188.9131\ \chi_4 + 6798.936\ \chi_5 + 1914.79\ \chi_6 + -21.8775\ \chi_7$$

APPENDIX 2 - <u>SYMBOLS USED:</u>

α = Apha (a)

β = Beta (b)

γ = Gamma (c)

ε = Epsilon (e)

μ = Mu (l)

χ = Chi (x)

Ho = Null Hypothesis

H_1 or Ha = Alternative Hypothesis

γ Variable = Dependent Variable or Response Variable

χ Variable = Independent Variable or Explanatory Variable or Predictor Variable

$\hat{y}$ = (y hat) added saturday26thseptember09)

Thank you!

Printed in Great Britain
by Amazon